KITCHEN GLASSWARE

of the Depression Years

Third Edition

By Gene Florence

Coordinated by Margaret Whitmyer

COLLECTOR BOOKS
A Division of Schroeder Publishing Co., Inc.

The current values in this book should be used only as a guide. They are not intended to set prices, which vary from one section of the country to another. Auction prices as well as dealer prices vary greatly and are affected by condition as well as demand. Neither the Author nor the Publisher assumes responsibility for any losses that might be incurred as a result of consulting this guide.

ABOUT THE AUTHOR

Gene Florence, born in Lexington in 1944, graduated from the University of Kentucky where he held a double major in mathematics and English. He taught nine years in the Kentucky school systems at the Junior High and High School levels before his glass collecting "hobby" became his full time job.

Mr. Florence has been interested in "collecting" since childhood, beginning with baseball cards and progressing through comic books, coins, bottles and finally, glassware. He first became interested in Depression glassware after purchasing a set of Sharon dinnerware at a garage sale for $5.00.

He has written several books on glassware: *The Collector's Encyclopedia of Depression Glass*, now in its seventh edition; *Elegant Glassware of the Depression Era*, now in its second edition; *The Collector's Encyclopedia of Akro Agate; The Collector's Encyclopedia of Occupied Japan*, Volume I, II and III and the *Pocket Guide to Depression Glass*, now in its fifth edition.

Should you be in Lexington, he is often found at Grannie Bear Antique Shop located at 120 Clay Avenue. This is the shop he helped his mother set up in what was formerly her children's day care center. The shop derived its name from the term of endearment the toddlers gave her.

Should you know of any unlisted or unusual pieces of kitchenware of the type mentioned in this book, you may write him at Box 22186, Lexington, KY 40522. If you expect a reply, you must enclose a self addressed, stamped envelope--and be patient. His travels and research often cause the hundreds of letters he receives weekly to backlog. He does appreciate your interest, however, and spends many hours answering your letters when time and circumstances permit.

ACKNOWLEDGMENTS

The culmination of three year's efforts to improve this book was vastly aided by several collectors and dealers who need special thanks--from those who shared collections to be photographed or aided in pricing, to those who helped in photographing or publishing. We all endeavoured to make this the best possible reflection of the collecting of kitchen glassware. The pictures, alone, in this book are the efforts of three photographers: Ziegfried Kurz (Ohio); Dave Hammell (California) and Dana Curtis (Kentucky).

A very special thanks to Kenn and Margaret Whitmyer and Terry and Celia McDuffee who opened their homes and lives for the invasion of a photography studio in order to show their vast collections of kitchenware to all you readers. They also helped in pricing and in giving moral support to get this mountainous task finished on time.

Nancy Maben deserves a special thanks for not only lending a large amount of her collection, but for helping in photographing and pricing. Thanks to the following for help in lending glass, photographing, or pricing information: Barbara and Kevin Kiley, Lorrie Kitchen and Dan Tucker, Sally Davis, Judy Smith, Jack Denny, Betty Franks, Don and Alice Huston, Steve Quertermous, Jane Fryberger, Janet Martin, Kirk Glauser, Sandy Tharp, Barbara Hammell and all those collectors who have written me or shared information at shows for the benefit of other collectors.

Thanks to the family, Cathy, Chad and Marc; Gene and Gladys Florence (Grannie Bear), and Charles and Sibyl Gaines who have endured the trials and tribulations of travel and deadlines which had to be met.

FOREWORD

In the three years since I wrote the second *Kitchen Glassware of the Depression Years*, I have been asked, over and over, "When is the next book coming out?" It was difficult to find enough new items to justify a new book until recently and that is why it took three years. As it was, I had to travel to the West Coast as well as use my ties nearer home to put this together.

The one thing I have observed is that more and more collectors are gathering kitchenware by colors than they are any other way. Because of this, the colors are the first listing in this book with the items and patterns following. Unfortunately, this has caused some overlapping of photos and information which my parcimonious nature decries, but it was done in order to please the collectors and not the author. In any case, you will note a very large color section this time with emphasis on green as you may have noted from the cover photo.

The most significant comment I have heard at shows concerns the availability of kitchenware. There are numerous pieces seen again and again, but the already harder to find items are showing up even less frequently. This happens in all fields of collecting. The choice pieces are bought up by serious collectors and until their collection is sold or broken up, many rarely found items are not on the market at any price. It takes patience as well as money to collect. One of the joys of collecting is finding that special piece that you have been seeking for a long time. It can make your day, week or even year!

You will note that the section on items such as sugar shakers and measuring cups has been widely expanded. In order to show you so many, I have been limited in my commentary. I have found that most of you are more interested in seeing as much glass as is possible, so I hope you will not be disappointed. It was not an easy job this time, and it will probably take another three or more years to do it again; so enjoy!

PRICING

All prices in this book are retail prices for mint condition glassware. This book is intended to be only a guide to the prices. A price range has been given for kitchenware items to allow for some wear and a little roughness that is normally not allowed in collecting other forms of Depression Glass. You will note that the price range has been widened in several areas but particularly in reamer and measuring cup collecting. I have received pricing ideas from over a dozen dealers and collectors and the range of pricing is enough to blow my mind. Since I, ultimately, must take the brunt of pricing discrepancies from collectors and dealers alike, I want you to know that the only rule in pricing seems to be determined by who owns it and who wishes to own it. In other words, only two people determine price, the buyer and the seller. You, ultimately, have to decide if the price is right for you.

The roughness or usage marks found on Kitchenware is a turn off to some collectors who search for perfection. Remember, these were utilitarian items and were in use for years; therefore, most collectors will allow some roughness. This does not mean cracks, chips and chunks are acceptable. To the contrary, these greatly reduce the value of a piece. It simply means that kitchenware collectors are a little more lenient about the condition of the glassware than are collectors of Depression dinnerware. They have to be because most of the kitchenware does not exist in absolutely mint condition!

I have seen both higher and lower prices for most items shown; however, the prices listed are prices that collectors somewhere in the country have been willing to pay.

COLORS

Anytime the word green or pink occurs, it means a transparent (see-through) color. Other color terms are described below.

Amethyst-a transparent, violet color
Black Amethyst-color appears black but will show purple under a strong light
Blue-"Chalaine," an opaque, sky blue made by McKee; "Cobalt," a transparent, dark blue; "Delphite," an opaque, medium blue made by Jeannette
Clambroth-translucent off white or translucent green

Custard-an opaque beige
Green-"Jad-ite," an opaque green made by Hocking; "Jadite," an opaque green made by Jeannette; "Skokie," an opaque green made by McKee
White-milk white; milk glass; opal white (All these terms simply indicate a white color); Vitrock, a white made by Hocking
Yellow-Vaseline, a transparent yellow; "Seville" yellow, an opaque yellow made by McKee

4

CONTENTS

PART 1 COLORS

AMBER (Dark)

Color has become the predominate way in which kitchenware is being collected. It has taken three books and suggestions from many readers to arrive at the format which I am now using. The book is divided into three sections: "Color", "Items", and "Patterns", in that order.

You will find many items shown in more than one place, in order to make them readily accessible for all the collectors of kitchenware.

There are still few collectors of amber, but many pieces are quite rare and will escalate in price if more demand is placed upon obtaining them. Only time will tell for sure, but sugar shakers and reamers in the darker shade of amber are some of the hardest to find. Item collectors are aware of this and now the secret is out.

ROW 1:	#1	Embossed "Coffee" canister	$ 60.00- 75.00
	#2	Embossed "Tea" canister	50.00- 65.00
	#3-6	Spice shakers, ea.	15.00- 20.00
	#7	Salt box	85.00-110.00
	#8	Measuring cup	125.00-150.00
ROW 2:	#1	Sugar canister	85.00-100.00
	#2	New Martinsville batter set	85.00-110.00
	#3	Cambridge etched grapes design ice bucket	30.00- 35.00
	#4	Valencia reamer, unembossed	150.00-200.00
ROW 3:	#1	Water bottle	30.00- 40.00
	#2-5	U.S. Glass mixing bowl set (4)	75.00- 90.00
		9″ bowl	25.00- 30.00
		8″ bowl	20.00- 22.50
		7″ bowl	17.50 20.00
		6″ bowl	12.50 15.00
ROW 4:	#1	Cake stand (fairly recent vintage)	12.50- 15.00
	#2	Fry reamer	200.00-250.00
	#3	Butter dish (foreign)	35.00- 50.00
	#4	Butter dish (similar to canisters above)	40.00- 55.00
ROW 5:	#1	Indiana Glass reamer	150.00-200.00
	#2	Fry oval tray	35.00- 45.00
	#3	Knife, 8¼″, "Stonex"	45.00- 55.00
	#4	Knife rest	15.00- 17.50
	#5	Apothecary measure, 1 oz.	20.00- 25.00

AMBER (Dark) Continued

First of all, there are a couple of items shown here that are not dark amber. Of note is the "Visible" mail box shown in the top row. Since the light amber was not going to be redone for this book, this box will give you a light piece to compare with the darker shade. The two piece Westmoreland reamer, shown in Row 3: #4, has still baffled me as to how it "jumped" into this picture. After all, it is shown on the next page under light amber; but maybe I should have let you find that goof!

The glass for this book was photographed at three different large photography sessions and several smaller ones. There were three different photographers from Ohio, California, and Kentucky involved and glass from all parts of the country; so please forgive the mistakes that slipped through. We worked as diligently as we could to give you an even better book than the last one.

The descriptions with all items shown are as complete as possible, but there is little space for me to do much writing in many areas. If it were a choice of seeing more glass or reading my words, the glass won every time.

I need to point out that drawer pulls come with two types of screws. Those with smaller screw backings are more collectible because they can be used with modern furniture without reaming larger holes.

ROW 1:	#1	Chesterfield pitcher	$ 50.00- 65.00
	#2	Chesterfield mug	15.00- 18.00
	#3	Imperial syrup	50.00 65.00
	#4	Sugar shaker	100.00-125.00
	#5	"Visible" mail box	50.00- 65.00
ROW 2:	#1	Cambridge oval covered casserole	20.00- 25.00
	#2	Cambridge covered casserole with underliner	18.00- 22.50
	#3	Cheese dish (possibly foreign)	40.00- 55.00
ROW 3:	#1	U.S. Glass 2 cup and reamer top	250.00-300.00
	#2	Cambridge 2-spouted gravy boat	22.50- 25.00
	#3	Cambridge footed cream sauce boat for asparagus platter	20.00- 22.50
	#4	Westmoreland 2-piece reamer	150.00-200.00
	#5	Lemon reamer (foreign)	85.00-100.00
	#6	Oil bottle	22.00- 25.00
ROW 4:	#1	Paden City "Party Line" ice bucket	22.00- 25.00
	#2	Same, 14 oz. tumbler	8.00- 10.00
	#3	Paden City egg cup	8.00- 9.00
	#4	Paden City hotel sugar and cover	20.00- 25.00
	#5	Paden City salt box	85.00-100.00
	#6	Cambridge oil bottle	35.00- 45.00
	#7	Tobacco jar	22.00- 25.00
ROW 5:	#1	"Feathered" curtain tie backs, pr.	17.50- 20.00
	#2	"Sandwich" round tie backs, pr.	15.00- 20.00
	#3	"Plume" tie backs or small round, pr.	15.00- 17.50
	#4	et. al. drawer pulls, ea. (large screws)	5.00- 7.00
		Same w/small screws	10.00- 12.50
	#5	Door knobs, set	50.00- 60.00

AMBER (Light) and BLACK

The shade of amber shown here is much easier to find than the darker shade. It is plentiful, but there are fewer collectors than for the dark. It is inexpensive, and you can purchase many ribbed pieces of amber Federal for less than you can buy newly made kitchenware. You may also note that the prices on the amber measuring cups have softened some, due to the abundance that has been found in relationship to the number of collectors searching for them.

The demand for unusual pieces of black kitchenware far outweighs the availability. Most collectors seem to want only a few pieces to decorate with instead of large accumulations as in other colors. I have been told that with several pieces of black a decor can be highlighted, whereas a quantity takes away this effect.

Page 11

ROW 1:

#1 Paden City "Party Line" reamer (2-piece) dark	$ 200.00-	250.00
#2 Tobacco jar	20.00-	22.50
#3 Reamer (2 piece), Westmoreland	150.00-	200.00
#4 Mug (Duncan Miller "Spiral Flutes")	15.00-	18.00

(Rows 2-5 are all Federal Glass Co. products except #3 in Row 2)

ROW 2:

#1 3 spout measure	30.00-	35.00
#2 3 spout handled measure	30.00-	35.00
#3 Chemical measure cup	20.00-	25.00
#4 Butter tub	20.00-	22.50
#5 Reamer	200.00-	300.00
#6 Refrigerator dish, 4" x 4"	6.00-	8.00

ROW 3:

#1 Refrigerator dish, 8" x 8"	$ 12.00-	14.00
#2 Butter dish (1 lb.)	25.00-	30.00
#3 Butter dish (¼ lb.)	22.00-	25.00
#4 Butter dish (¼ lb.)	22.00-	25.00

ROW 4:

#1 Refrigerator dish, 4" x 8"	8.00-	10.00
#2 Bowl, 6"	4.00-	5.00
#3 Bowl, 8"	5.00-	6.00
#4 Bowl, 11¼", flared rim, set of 6 (see below)	27.00-	33.00
Same, 10¾" (not shown)	6.00-	7.00

ROW 5:

#1 Same, 9¾"	5.00-	6.00
#2 Same, 8¾"	4.00-	5.00
#3 Same, 7¾"	3.00-	4.00
#4 Same, 6¾"	2.00-	3.00

BLACK

Page 12

ROW 1:

#1 Sellers sugar canister	$ 50.00-	55.00
#2 Salt or pepper, ea.	12.00-	15.00
#3 McKee batter jug	50.00-	60.00
#4 Cocktail shaker	25.00-	30.00
#5 Syrup, covered	40.00-	50.00

ROW 2:

#1 McKee, 4½" salt (harder to find than pepper)	10.00-	12.00
Same, pepper (weak lettering-50% of prices)	8.00-	10.00
Same, flour or sugar	10.00-	12.00
#2 McKee, 3½" sugar (priced as above)	12.00-	14.00
#3 Covered ice bucket	40.00-	50.00
#4 McKee tumbler	15.00-	18.00
#5 Straw in tumbler	3.00-	4.00
#6 Paden City batter jug set	160.00-	185.00

ROW 3:

All shakers priced as in ROW 2 with those having badly worn or missing lettering 50% of prices listed) EXCEPT last pr.	$ 30.00-	35.00

ROW 4:

#1 Butter dish w/crystal top (possibly foreign)	50.00-	65.00
#2 Egg cup	10.00-	12.50
#3 Drawer pull, double	12.00-	15.00
#4 Paden City "Party Line" napkin holder	80.00-	100.00
#5 Nar-O-Fold Napkin Company Chicago, U.S.A.	80.00-	100.00

ROW 5:

#1 Punch ladle	40.00-	55.00
#2-5 Drawer pulls, ea.	8.00-	10.00
#3 Cambridge salad set	60.00-	75.00

Page 13

ROW 1:

#1 L.E. Smith Co. cookie jar	$ 35.00-	40.00
#2 L.E. Smith Co. cookier jar	30.00-	35.00
#3 L.E. Smith Co. bowl and lid	35.00-	40.00

ROW 2:

#1 Paden City batter set w/tray	85.00-	100.00
#2 Reamer, two part, oval shaped "Tricia"	400.00-	500.00
#3,4 Salt & pepper, pr.	35.00-	40.00

ROW 3:

#1 Bowl, 8⅜"	$ 20.00-	24.00
Bowl, 9⅜" (not shown)	25.00-	28.00
#2 Bowl, 7⅜"	18.00-	20.00
#3 Bowl, 6⅜"	15.00-	16.00
#4 Bowl, 5⅜"	12.00-	15.00

ROW 4:

#1 McKee bowl, 7⅜" w/holder	20.00-	25.00
#2 Bowl, crushed fruit w/ladle & lid	30.00-	40.00
#3 Bowl, 5" (rarely seen)	18.00-	20.00

BLUE (CHALAINE) and PEACOCK BLUE

Chalaine blue, shown on page 15 and 16, has become an even more popular color of kitchenware since appearing on the cover of the 2ND Edition. Unfortunately, there is little available for the large demand. You can tell from the prices which pieces are desirable and rare. In fact, if you find any additional pieces, just let me know.

Peacock Blue on page 17 is not as avidly sought, but the canisters in Row 2 are quite an addition to any collection.

Page 15

ROW 1:
#1-4 Canisters (press-on lids), ea.	$ 90.00-110.00
#5 Refrigerator dish, 4″ x 5″	
(shown stacked) ea.	30.00- 35.00

ROW 2:
#1-4 Shakers, ea.	22.50- 25.00
#5 Shaker, nutmeg	40.00- 45.00
#6 Sunkist reamer	125.00-155.00

ROW 3:
#1 Butter dish, plain, no tabs	225.00-250.00
#2 Butter dish, ribbed, tab	
handles	200.00-225.00
#3 Ginger (?) jar	25.00- 30.00

ROW 4:
#1 Measure pitcher, 4 cup	$100.00-125.00
#2 Measure cup, 2 spout	350.00-450.00
#3 Rolling pin, shaker top	250.00-300.00

ROW 5:
#1 Refrigerator dish, 7¼″ sq.	75.00- 85.00
#2 Toothbrush holder	20.00- 25.00
#3 Towel bar, 17″	25.00- 30.00
#4 Drawer pull, double	12.00- 15.00
#5 Drawer pull, single	6.00- 10.00

Page 16

ROW 1:
#1 Pitcher, ftd. (possibly Fenton)	$125.00-150.00
#2 Measure pitcher, 4 cup	350.00-400.00
#3-5 Canisters, screw-on lids	90.00-110.00

ROW 2:
#1 Canister, rnd, 48 oz., blue lid	45.00- 55.00
#2 Canister, rnd, 24 oz., blue lid	30.00- 37.50
#3 Canister, rnd, 10 oz., blue lid	30.00- 37.50

ROW 3:
#1 Beater bowl, w/spout, 4½″	
tall	25.00- 30.00
#2 Beater bowl, w/spout, 4″ tall	25.00- 30.00

ROW 3: (Continued)
#3 Grapefruit reamer	$250.00-300.00
#4 Egg cup	10.00- 12.00

ROW 4:
#1 Mixing bowl, 9″	40.00- 50.00
#2 Bowl, 7½″	30.00- 35.00
#3 Bowl, 6″	22.50- 25.00

ROW 5:
#1,2 Salt box (2 shades)	125.00-150.00
#3 Shakers, (2 shades) embossed	
print (flour $40.00-45.00)	
others	55.00- 60.00

PEACOCK BLUE

Page 17

ROW 1:
#1 Strawholder (probably 1950's)	$150.00-200.00
#2 L.E. Smith cookie jar	50.00- 60.00
#3 Imperial decanter	20.00- 25.00
#4 Dispenser (possibly sugar)	150.00-200.00

ROW 2:
#1 Sugar, 5 lb. canister	150.00-175.00
#2 Coffee, 40 oz. canister	85.00-100.00
#3 Tea, 20 oz. canister	70.00- 85.00
#4-6 Shakers, 8 oz., ea.	40.00- 50.00
#7 Salt box	100.00-125.00

ROW 3:
#1 Ice tub	20.00- 25.00
#2 Rolling pin	125.00-150.00
#3 Mug	22.00- 25.00

ROW 4:
#1 Jar (paper label, sold by route	
merchants)	$ 10.00- 12.50
#2-8 Tie backs, large pr.	20.00- 25.00
small pr.	15.00- 20.00

ROW 5:
#1,3 Towel rods, ea.	20.00- 25.00
#2 Double towel rod	25.00- 30.00

ROW 6:
#1,2 Spoons, ea.	8.00- 12.00
#3,4 Salad set	35.00- 45.00
#5,6 Double drawer pulls, ea.	18.00- 20.00
#7-11 Single drawer pulls, ea.	10.00- 12.00

BLUE (COBALT)

Demand for cobalt blue in any form has always been tremendous; but avid collectors would almost "kill" for a kitchen decorated in this color. Desirable pieces are the canisters, sugar shakers, rolling pins and reamers, but many collectors would settle for anything.

Page 19 All Hazel Atlas except last row.

ROW 1:

#1-5 Canister w/lid (deduct $50.00-75.00 for worn lettering)		$200.00-250.00

ROW 2:

#1 2 Cup measure w/reamer top	200.00-250.00
#2 Tab handled orange reamer	175.00-200.00
#3 Tab handled lemon reamer	250.00-300.00
#4 Milk pitcher	40.00- 50.00
#5 1 Cup measure, 3 spout	300.00-350.00

ROW 3:

#1 Stack refrigerator, 4½" x 5", ea.	35.00- 40.00
#2 Round refrigerator, 5¾"	40.00- 45.00
#3 Water bottle, 64 oz., 10" tall	50.00- 55.00
#4 Hazel Atlas bottle, (possibly medicinal)	15.00- 20.00
#5 Mixer, Vidrio Products	75.00-100.00

ROW 4:

#1 Butter dish	$125.00-150.00
#2 Bowl, 5¾", "Restwell"	10.00- 12.00
#3 Bowl, 6"	10.00- 12.00
#4 Tumbler, marked HA	10.00- 15.00

ROW 5:

#1 Spoon stirrer	6.00- 8.00
#2 Curtain tie back	12.00- 15.00
#3 Drawer pull	8.00- 10.00
#4,5 Stirrers, ea.	1.00- 1.50
#6-8 Spoon or forks, ea.	17.50- 22.50
#9 Coaster	4.00- 5.00

Page 20

ROW 1:

#1 Bowl, 8½" (add $5.00 w/metal)	$ 12.00- 15.00
#2 Bowl, 7⅝" (add $5.00 w/metal)	15.00- 18.00
#3 Bowl, 6⅝" (add $5.00 w/metal)	12.00- 15.00

ROW 2:

#1 Bowl, 9⅝" (add $5.00 w/metal)	20.00- 22.50
#2 Bowl, 10⅝"	35.00- 40.00
#3 Bowl, 11⅝" (all of above are Hazel Atlas)	40.00- 50.00

ROW 3:

#1 L.E. Smith water dispenser	$250.00-300.00
#2 Cambridge mug	35.00- 50.00
#3 Shakers, pr. (possibly bath powder)	15.00- 18.00

ROW 4:

#1 L.E. Smith bowl, 8¼"	35.00- 40.00
#2 Same, 7¼"	30.00- 35.00
#3 Same, 6¼"	25.00- 30.00

ROW 5:

#1 Mustard pot	20.00- 25.00
#2 Fry cake plate, 3 ftd.	50.00- 60.00
#3,4 Fork and spoon, set	35.00- 45.00

Page 21

ROW 1:

#1 Barbell cocktail shaker	$ 60.00- 75.00
#2 Strawholder	150.00-200.00
#3 Cocktail shaker	30.00- 35.00
#4 McKee batter jug	65.00- 80.00

ROW 2:

#1 New Martinsville batter set	225.00-250.00
#2,3 Shakers w/blue tops	25.00- 35.00
#4 Sugar shaker (older than Depression era)	125.00-150.00
#5 Sugar shaker	200.00-250.00
#6 Tumble up	35.00- 40.00

ROW 3:

#1 Paden City batter jug	40.00- 45.00
#2 Same, milk jug	35.00- 40.00
#3 Same, syrup jug	30.00- 35.00
#4 Cambridge reamer	1500.00-2000.00

ROW 4:

#1 Cobalt rolling pin	225.00- 275.00
#2 Cobalt handles rolling pin	150.00- 175.00

BLUE (Delphite) JEANNETTE GLASS CO., LATE '30's

You will note that the prices for almost every piece in this color have increased since the last book. This is not that unusual over a three-year period except that it has been both demand from collectors and scarcity of this color that have increased the price. Dealers have even found a way to sell the "Matches" holder without lettering on it! It is being marketed as an egg cup by enterprising entrepreneurs.

One development in the collecting of shakers has been the discovery that the round shakers marked "flour", "sugar" and "paprika" are not as poorly distributed as once believed, although on the West Coast the "flour" seems to be harder to find. In the square shakers the "flour" and "sugar" are still harder to find than the "salt" or "pepper"; but for these there is not as much price differentiation as in the round shakers.

I have listed several other bowls since last time for those of you who requested that I do so.

One question that I have been asked several times concerns the one cup in the measuring set. This cup has a spout which points directly at you if you hold it in your right hand. There is no spout on the jadite and this has caused some confusion for beginning collectors.

ROW 1:	#1	Canister, 40 oz., coffee	$85.00- 95.00
	#2	Same, sugar	90.00-100.00
	#3	Canister, 20 oz., tea	60.00- 75.00
	#4-6	Shaker, 8 oz., sugar, flour, paprika	18.00- 20.00
	#7	Bud vase	10.00- 12.50
	#8	Bowl w/metal beater	25.00- 30.00
ROW 2:	#1,3	Shaker, salt or pepper	10.00- 12.50
	#2	Drippings bowl, w/lettering	30.00- 35.00
		w/o lettering	12.00- 15.00
	#4-7	Canisters, square, 29 oz., 5″, w/lid, ea.	45.00- 55.00
ROW 3:	#1	Butter dish	85.00-100.00
	#2	Refrigerator dish, 4″ x 4″	12.00- 15.00
		Same, 4″ x 8″	20.00- 25.00
	#3,4	Salt or pepper	12.00- 15.00
	#5,6	Flour or sugar	20.00- 25.00
	#7	Measuring cup set (4)	85.00-100.00
		1 cup	35.00- 40.00
		½ cup	25.00- 30.00
		⅓ cup	15.00- 17.50
		¼ cup	10.00- 12.50
ROW 4:	#1	Round 32 oz. refrigerator bowl	27.00- 30.00
	#2	Measure pitcher, 2 cup, (Sunflower in bottom)	35.00- 40.00
	#3	Crushed fruit bowl	60.00- 75.00
	#4	"Matches" holder, w/lettering	25.00- 30.00
		Same, w/o lettering (sold as egg cup)	15.00- 18.00
	#5	Electric beater	35.00- 40.00
ROW 5:	#1-3	Mixing bowl set (4)	85.00-100.00
		9″ bowl	25.00- 30.00
		8″ bowl	20.00- 25.00
		7″ bowl	18.00- 20.00
		6″ bowl (rare)	22.00- 25.00
	#4	Mixing bowl, horizontal ribs, 7½″	32.00- 35.00
		Same, 9¾″ (not shown)	45.00- 50.00
		Same, 5½″ (not shown)	22.00- 25.00

BLUE DELPHITE and BLUE MISCELLANEOUS

There is so little delphite McKee available that it is almost uncollectable. The last two pieces in the top row are questionable as to maker but they match so well that I have included them here. All the other pieces in the first three rows are McKee with the exception of the ash tray which might even be Pyrex made by Corning.

The last two rows only have "blue" color as a common denominator, but there are some interesting pieces shown there. The "cornflower blue" Fry reamer was borrowed too late to be included with the rest of the reamers, but it is better to see it here than no place at all. The L.E. Smith bowls and the "Block Optic" butter dish were shown last time but were again worthy of inclusion. At this point in time, the blue butter is still the only complete one known.

In the bottom row is a Paden City cotton ball dispenser in the form of a bunny. The next cotton ball to be used forms her tail. A clever idea and definitely pre-Playboy days.

Notice the Peacock Blue scoop that missed its respective page, but its color is appreciated here too.

ROW 1:	#1	McKee measure pitcher, 4 cup	$225.00-275.00
	#2	McKee measure pitcher, 2 cup	40.00- 55.00
	#3	McKee 48 oz. round canister	45.00- 55.00
	#4	McKee 10 oz. round canister	30.00- 35.00
	#5	Vase	20.00- 25.00
	#6	Ginger (?) jar	15.00- 18.00
ROW 2:	#1	McKee butter dish	100.00-125.00
	#2	McKee refrigerator dish, 4" x 5"	22.50- 25.00
	#3,4	Shakers, ea.	25.00- 30.00
	#5	Ash tray, possibly McKee or Pyrex	12.00- 15.00
ROW 3:	#1	Mixing bowl, 9"	30.00- 40.00
	#2	Mixing bowl, 7⅜"	25.00- 30.00
	#3	Bowl w/spout, 4¼"	20.00- 25.00
	#4	Bowl, 4⅜" (cocotte)	12.50- 15.00
ROW 4:	#1	L.E. Smith, 9¼" bowl	40.00- 50.00
	#2	L.E. Smith, 7" bowl	30.00- 35.00
	#3	Fry, cornflower blue reamer	300.00-350.00
	#4	Hocking, "Block Optic" butter dish	350.00-400.00
ROW 5:	#1	Cheese dish (possibly foreign)	60.00- 75.00
	#2	Scoop	35.00- 40.00
	#3	Paden City bunny, cotton ball dispenser	40.00- 50.00
	#4	Soap dish, "Home Soap Company"	22.50- 25.00

"CLAMBROTH" WHITE

"Clambroth" white refers to this washed out, translucent white color shown on page 27. Remember this is a collector's descriptive name and not that of any one company that made glassware during the Depression Era. For example, the reamer shown was made by MacBeth-Evans and the covered casserole in the next row is Corning's Pyrex.

In Row 4 there is a ladle that was used in two vastly different ways. With a hole in the bottom it was considered a pickle dipper and allowed the brine to drain away when you scooped out a pickle. With the hole plugged by a metal piece and measurements on the side it was considered a dry measure. Maybe it was used to measure the ingredients for the brine while pickling at home and later turned into the dipper for the barrel of homemade sweet pickles.

As reported last time, a refrigerator water dispenser in "clambroth" white has also been found. It sells in the $60.00-70.00 range.

Although there is not an abundance of this color available, there are few collectors at present.

ROW 1:	#1	Canister, large	$ 22.00- 25.00
	#2	Canister, medium	20.00- 22.00
	#3-5	Canister, embossed, "TEA," "SUGAR," "FLOUR," ea.	30.00- 32.00
ROW 2:	#1,2	Salt or pepper, ea.	12.00- 15.00
	#3	Sugar canister w/label	22.00- 25.00
	#4	Coffee canister w/label	20.00- 22.00
	#5	Canister w/o label	12.00- 15.00
	#6,7	Shakers w/o label, ea.	8.00- 10.00
ROW 3:	#1	Barber bottle	5.00- 6.00
	#2	Rolling pin	125.00-135.00
	#3	MacBeth-Evans reamer	300.00-350.00
ROW 4:	#1	Pyrex casserole	25.00- 30.00
	#2	Oval dish	5.00- 8.00
	#3	Bowl, round (has screw-on lid)	7.00- 10.00
	#4	Pickle dipper	15.00- 18.00
ROW 5:	#1	Refrigerator drip tray	7.00- 10.00
	#2,3	Salt or pepper, ea.	10.00- 12.00
	#4	Sugar shaker (1 large hole in top)	35.00- 37.50

CRYSTAL

Many collectors turn up their noses at these crystal pieces. However, they are very practical for use in today's modern kitchens. The "Dutch" canisters hold flour (3 kinds) and rice on a wall shelf in our kitchen. The other "Dutch" shakers in Row 3 adorn a couple of other shelves. The cocoa was left in #6 to show it is really used. Besides, washing all those ingredients out every time is a pain. I don't recommend using these items in an automatic dishwasher if you care to see them with designs on them at their next use.

The clothes sprinkler leaning up on the back row has the original cardboard instructions attached—"K.R. Haley Glassware Co., Inc., Greensburg, Penn. This sprinkler is excellent for sprinkling flours, watering plants and for sprinkling insecticides on flowers and shrubs as well as for dampening clothes". "Does not leak without shaking".

In addition to the three markings for spoon measures of tea, dessert, and table, the measure in Row 4: #3 is marked "Edward Kipp, Pharmacist 3000 Colerain Ave."

Page 29

ROW 1:	#1	McKee Glasbake Scientific Measuring cup	$15.00-	20.00
	#2-5	Hocking canister w/Dutch decal	12.00-	15.00
	#6	Pint measure in tablespoons for coffee, tea and wine	10.00-	12.50
ROW 2:	#1,2	John Alden (salt) and Priscilla (pepper), pr.	17.50-	20.00
	#3	Westmoreland baby reamer w/decal	35.00-	40.00
	#4	Horseradish jar	10.00-	12.50
	#5	Salt box	12.00-	15.00
	#6	Toast holder	35.00-	40.00
	#7	Spoon holder (Pat. Feb. 11, 1913)	15.00-	18.00
ROW 3:	#1-10	Dutch shakers (12 or 16 oz.), ea. (Cocoa in 6th)	7.50-	9.00
ROW 4:	#1	Flour canister, 128 oz.	20.00-	25.00
	#2	Coffee dripolater	10.00-	12.50
	#3	Measure spoon (markings for table, dessert, tea)	4.00-	5.00
	#4	Sprinkler (leaning in back) cardboard wrapped instructions	17.50-	20.00
	#5	Heisey sugar cube tray	30.00-	35.00
	#6	Jiffy one cupper coffee maker w/filter	8.00-	10.00

Page 30

ROW 1:	#1	Canister, coffee	12.00-	15.00
	#2	Canister, tea	10.00-	12.00
	#3	Canister	12.00-	15.00
	#4	Set (5 piece on rack)	35.00-	40.00
		Large canister	20.00-	25.00
		Shakers, ea.	4.00-	5.00
ROW 2:	#1	Set (9 piece on rack)	40.00-	45.00
	#2	Canister w/Dutch decal	12.00-	15.00
	#3	Canister w/"Taverne" scene	18.00-	20.00
ROW 3:	#1,2	Shakers, handled, ea.	6.50-	7.50
	#3	Canister, tall coffee	14.00-	16.00
	#4	Canister, coffee	12.00-	14.00
	#5	Canister, tea	10.00-	12.00
	#6	Salt box	12.00-	15.00
ROW 4:	#1,2	Round horizontal ribbed canister, large	14.00-	16.00
		Same, medium	8.00-	10.00
	#3	Canister, large ribbed	22.00-	25.00

Page 31

ROW 1:	#1-4	Owens-Illinois Ovoid shape set (6) w/good labels	40.00-	50.00
		Coffee	12.00-	15.00
		Tea	10.00-	12.00
		Shakers, ea.	5.00-	6.00
	#5,6	Figural shaker, odd, uneven bottom, pr.	15.00-	18.00
ROW 2:	#1-4	Barrel shaped canister, large	12.00-	15.00
		Same, medium	10.00-	12.00
		Same, shakers, ea.	5.00-	6.00
	#5-7	Shakers, ea.	3.00-	4.00
ROW 3:	#1	Frosted coffee canister, Owens-Illinois	12.00-	15.00
	#2	Frosted tea canister	12.00-	15.00
	#3	Hazel Atlas canister (like cobalt blue pg. 129)	12.00-	15.00
	#4	Shaker, Kroger peanut butter label	4.00-	5.00
	#5	Shakers, bottom fill "moisture proof" w/metal inserts	35.00-	40.00
	#6	Round refrigerator jar "lattice" design	7.00-	8.00
ROW 4:	#1-4	Hocking "Tulip" pattern lid canisters, ea. (50's)	4.00-	5.00
	#5,6	Shakers, 2 styles of "Quaker" or "Zipper," ea.	5.00-	8.00
	#7	Shakers (Lavarro pineapple syrup label), ea.	4.00-	5.00
		Same (no labels), ea.	1.50-	2.00

CUSTARD, McKEE GLASS COMPANY

For those of you who are beginning to collect, I should point out that this color is available in today's market. Some of the other colors do not seem to turn up as often. Because of availability, the prices are somewhat more reasonable than the blues, greens or pinks. Of course, there are many who do not like opaque colors because the contents of the containers can't be viewed. I think this is an attractive kitchenware color, however.

Rolling pins have become more plentiful than once thought. In fact, at a recent show I attended, four were being offered for sale. That was an unusual circumstance, but it does point out that our ideas on supply sometimes have to be adjusted. This also leads to price adjustments, and those who buy and sell have to keep up with all these considerations.

The "Sunkist" reamer in custard was well distributed and is still plentiful; so, be sure that you can distinguish this color from the many rarer shades. In Row 4 the water bottle is quite unusual, but the style has never seemed to catch on with collectors possibly because it's hard to grip. Picture your child trying to pour from this!

ROW 1:	#1	Canister, 48 oz., tea	$ 25.00- 30.00
	#2	Ribbed canister, coffee (rare)	35.00- 40.00
	#3	Canister, round w/lid, 48 oz.	18.00- 20.00
	#4	Same, 46 oz.	15.00- 18.00
	#5	Challenge mixer	20.00- 25.00
ROW 2:	#1	Measure pitcher, 32 oz.	20.00- 25.00
	#2-4	Shakers, ea.	8.00- 10.00
	#5	Refrigerator water dispenser	85.00-100.00
ROW 3:	#1	Triangular refrigerator dish	10.00- 12.00
	#2	Butter dish w/green stripe	35.00- 45.00
	#3	Salt and pepper (plastic base custard color)	4.00- 5.00
	#4	Salt bowl	50.00- 60.00
ROW 4:	#1	Juice or egg cup	4.00- 5.00
	#2	Sunkist reamer	22.00- 25.00
	#3-8	Shakers, ea. ("Roman" arch side panel)	8.00- 10.00
ROW 5:	#1	Shaker, square, nutmeg	18.00- 20.00
	#2	Shaker, red lettering	12.00- 15.00
	#3	Rolling pin, shaker end, ridge handle	125.00-150.00
	#4	Rolling pin, shaker end, smooth handle	125.00-150.00
	#5	Water bottle	100.00-110.00
ROW 6:	#1	Butter dish (arches and tab handles)	30.00- 35.00
	#2	Tray, 11", round	15.00- 18.00
	#3	Oval bowl, 7"	12.00- 15.00

FOREST GREEN

There are several interesting items pictured here. In the top row on the right are McKee pieces. The syrup and the oil bott set go together although the oil set seems to photograph a lighter color than the syrup. These are probably late 1940's, b are not a common McKee color. The embossed "COFFEE" (Row 2: #4) has a flip-up top for easier pouring. If the original ca is missing, deduct $10.00-12.00 off the price listed. The sugar shaker (Row 4: #4) seems to be a late 1950's, early 1960's issu It was made in all the right colors such as red and cobalt blue also. The bottom row shows the only Forest Green rolling pi I have seen; the pair of curtain rings are also unusual in this color. The Green "Clambroth" shown on pages 36 and 37 is th collectors name for this pale, shimmery, translucent-edged green made by Hocking and others at that time. The bottom tw rows on page 37 are not Green "Clambroth" but unusual jadite items leading into the next section.

Page 35

ROW 1:

#1	Owens-Illinois vinegar or water bottle w/tray	$ 25.00-	30.00
	Same w/o tray	10.00-	12.50
#2	Hocking water bottle w/top	17.50-	20.00
#3	Duraglas water bottle	20.00-	25.00
#4	McKee syrup (goes with #5)	25.00-	30.00
#5	Oil and Vinegar set (goes w/#4)	15.00-	20.00

ROW 2:

#1,2	Owens-Illinois canisters (ovoid shape), ea.	20.00-	25.00
	Same, TEA (not shown)	15.00-	18.00
#3	Same, shaker size	8.00-	10.00
	Prices for above 30% to 40% less w/missing lettering		
#4	Owens-Illinois embossed COF-FEE w/flip top	32.50-	37.50

ROW 2 (continued)

#5	Owens-Illinois water bottle	$ 12.50-	15.00

ROW 3:

#1-3	Owens-Illinois 40 oz. diagonal ridged canister, ea.	15.00-	17.50
#4-5	Same 20 oz., ea. (TEA, RICE)	10.00-	12.50
#6	Same 10 oz.	6.00-	8.00
#7,8	Shakers, ea.	5.00-	6.00

ROW 4:

#1	New Martinsville batter jug	40.00-	50.00
#2	Same, syrup jug	30.00-	40.00
#3	Cruet	30.00-	35.00
#4	Sugar shaker (1950's)	45.00-	60.00

ROW 5:

#1,2	Curtain rings, ea.	8.00-	10.00
#3	Rolling pin	125.00-	150.00
#4,5	Shakers, pr.	12.00-	15.00

GREEN CLAMBROTH

Page 36

ROW 1:

#1-4	Hocking canisters w/glass lid, 47 oz., ea.	$ 32.00-	35.00
#5-8	Hocking shakers, 8 oz. ea.	12.00-	15.00

ROW 2:

#1	Hocking oval refrig. dish, 8"	30.00-	35.00
#2	Same, 7"	22.00-	25.00
#3	Same, 6"	15.00-	18.00
#4	Refrigerator jar, 4¼" x 4¾"	20.00-	22.50
#5	Hocking drippings jar (possibly powder jar)	15.00-	20.00
#6	Hocking 2 cup measure	85.00-	100.00

ROW 3:

#1	Hocking 1 cup measure	100.00-	150.00
#2	Hocking reamer	75.00-	100.00
#3	Fenton reamer top for pitcher	75.00-	100.00
#4	Jadite Sunkist (there is one that is much more translucent than this)	15.00-	22.50

ROW 3 (Continued)

#5	Cold cream jar	$ 12.00-	15.00
#6	Mug	25.00-	30.00

ROW 4:

#1	Owl "tumble-up" nite set (pitcher and glass as top)	85.00-	100.00
#2	Butter dish	40.00-	50.00
#3	McKee Hall's refrigerator dish, 4" x 6"	10.00-	14.00
#4	Water dispenser w/crystal top	45.00-	55.00

ROW 5:

#1	Ice bucket	35.00-	40.00
#2	Whipped cream pail	30.00-	35.00
#3	Fenton pitcher missing lid (as pictured)	40.00-	50.00
#4	Towel bar holders, pr.	20.00-	25.00
#5	Sugar shaker	20.00-	25.00
#6	"Serv-All" napkin holder	75.00-	100.00

Page 37

ROW 1:

#1	Pitcher (Fenton?)	$ 50.00-	60.00
#2	Tumbler to match above	8.00-	10.00
#3	Fenton ice bucket and lid	75.00-	85.00
#4	Tumbler, ftd.	10.00-	12.00
#5	Sherbet	6.00-	7.50
#6	Door knob set	35.00-	45.00

ROW 2:

#1	Mixing bowl, 8¾"	15.00-	20.00
#2	Same, 7¾"	12.00-	15.00
#3	Same, 6¾"	10.00-	12.00
#4	Powder shaker ?	15.00-	18.00

ROW 3:

#1	Ash tray	4.00-	5.00
#2	Wall tumbler holder	8.00-	10.00
#3	Coaster	8.00-	10.00
#4	Furniture "foot rest" (per 1920's Montgomery Ward catalogue)	4.00-	5.00

ROW 3 (Continued)

#5	Jadite towel bar in rear	$ 20.00-	25.00
#6	Soap dish	12.00-	15.00
#7	Jade ash tray	4.00-	5.00
#8	Jade makeup holder	12.00-	15.00

ROW 4:

#1,2	Canisters, fired-on, ea.	30.00-	35.00
#3	Decanter, pinched	85.00-	100.00
#4	Water bottle	85.00-	100.00
#5	Bowl, 4¾" twist design	10.00-	12.00
#6	McKee bottoms up w/coaster (coaster $40.00-50.00)	70.00-	80.00

ROW 5:

#1	Jade vinegar cruet	65.00-	75.00
#2	Refrigerator dish, wedge shaped	15.00-	20.00
#3	Refrigerator w/jade lid	8.00-	10.00
#4	Cigarette ash tray	12.00-	15.00
#5	Bowl, 4½"	8.00-	10.00

GREEN JADITE

Pages 39 and 40 show only Jeannette's "Jadite". There are many shades of this ware and this creates problems for collectors trying to match their purchases if buying by mail. Be sure to specify light or dark if that is what you want. The lids for the 3″ spice jars shown in Row 2 are difficult to find. Try to pick a lid from one and you will see why!

Page 39

ROW 1:	#1-4	Canister, square, 48 oz., "Floral" design inside lid, ea.	$ 22.00-	25.00
	#5	Refrigerator dish, 5″ x 5″, "Floral" design inside lid	16.00-	18.00
		Same, 10″ x 5″	26.00-	28.00
ROW 2:	#1	Batter jug w/lid	125.00-	150.00
	#2	Salt box	100.00-	125.00
	#3,4	Canister, square, 29 oz., lettered or plain	18.00-	20.00
	#5	Canister, square, 3″ spice, ea.	18.00-	20.00
ROW 3:	#1	Refrigerator dish, 4″ x 4″	8.00-	10.00
		Same, 8″ x 4″	12.00-	15.00
	#2,3	Shakers, Flour or Sugar	10.00-	12.00
	#4,5	Shakers, Salt or Pepper	8.00-	10.00
	#6	Reamer, dark	30.00-	35.00
		Same, light (not shown)	15.00-	18.00
	#7	Sugar shaker, yellow shade	40.00-	50.00
	#8	Reamer, yellow shade	75.00-	90.00
ROW 4:	#1-3	Mixing bowl set (4 sizes)	33.00-	38.00
		9″	10.00-	12.00
		8″, (not shown)	9.00-	10.00
		7″	8.00-	9.00
		6″	6.00-	7.00
	#4	Pitcher	20.00-	22.00

Page 40

ROW 1:	#1-3	Canister, round, screw-on lid, 40 oz., ea.	22.00-	25.00
	#4	Same, 16 oz.	16.00-	18.00
	#5-8	Shakers, round, 8 oz., ea.	8.00-	10.00
ROW 2:	#1	Round crock, 40 oz., knob on top, desirable	30.00-	35.00
	#2	Round refrigerator dish, 32 oz.	15.00-	18.00
	#3	Butter dish	30.00-	35.00
	#4-8	Shakers, round, 6 oz., w/label, ea.	7.00-	8.00
		Shakers, w/o label	4.00-	5.00
ROW 3:	#1-4	Measuring cup set (4)	33.00-	43.00
		1 cup	12.00-	15.00
		½ cup	10.00-	12.50
		⅓ cup	6.00-	8.00
		¼ cup	5.00-	7.50
	#5	Drip jar (no lettering)	5.00-	6.00
		Same, w/lettering (not shown)	20.00-	23.00
	#6	Measure pitcher, 2 cup	10.00-	12.00
	#7	Beater bowl (w/beater)	8.00-	10.00
ROW 4:	#1	Mixing bowl, ribbed, 9¾″	25.00-	30.00
	#2	Same, 7½″	12.00-	15.00
	#3	Same, 5½″	8.00-	10.00
	#4	Lemon reamer, light	12.00-	15.00

Page 41

ROW 1:	#1	"Lady" flour	15.00-	17.50
	#2-6	Shakers, ea.	10.00-	12.50
	#7,8	Cone shaker, pr.	10.00-	12.50
	#9-11	Embossed shakers, (flour or sugar $30.00-35.00); pepper	28.00-	30.00
ROW 2:	#1	Tab handled, 9½″ mixing bowl	8.00-	10.00
	#2	Spouted, 6½″, mixing bowl	6.00-	8.00
	#3	Water dispenser, Jadite top	35.00-	45.00
ROW 3:	#1	9″ bowl lettered J. Grosso Market	18.00-	20.00
	#2	9″ bowl (not for electric mixer)	15.00-	18.00
	#3	Salt bowl	75.00-	85.00
	#4	Shakers, plastic Jadite colored bottom	5.00-	6.00
ROW 4:	#1	Complete mixer (never been used); In original box	55.00-	75.00

GREEN JADITE, McKEE GLASS CO., (CALLED SKOKIE GREEN BY McKEE)

"Skokie Green" is the name given to the opaque green of McKee, but collectors have never been fond of that name. Jadite is the name that all opaque green is lumped into for simplicity, if for no other reason. There are a few harder-to-find items pictured, but there is nothing here that is really rare.

The hard-to-find category includes the columned canisters and 4 cup measure without handles in Row 1. Row 3 has a two spouted cup measure that is extremely rare in other colors, but is found more frequently in Jadite.

The "Bottoms Down" beer mug in Row 4 is highly sought by glassware collectors as well as collectors of mugs and nudes.

As in the custard color, the water bottle shown in Row 5 is unusual, but has never caught on with collectors as have the other styles of water bottles.

ROW 1:	#1-4	Canisters, 28 oz., square, ea.	$ 32.00- 35.00
	#5	Measure pitcher, 4 cup	20.00- 25.00
	#6	Columned canister, 48 oz. (rare)	45.00- 50.00
	#7	Same, 20 oz.	35.00- 38.00
	#8	Measure pitcher (sans handle), 4 cup	125.00-150.00
ROW 2:	#1	Refrigerator dish, 4" x 5"	9.00- 10.00
		Same, 8" x 5"	12.00- 14.00
	#2-5	Shakers, ea.	8.00- 10.00
	#6	"Soap Powder," unusual label	25.00- 30.00
	#7	Refrigerator water dispenser	75.00- 85.00
ROW 3:	#1	Butter dish	30.00- 35.00
	#2	2 spout measure cup	85.00-100.00
	#3-5	Shakers, "Roman" arch side panel, ea. (spice $22.00-25.00)	12.00- 15.00
	#6	Covered coaster holder for 6 coasters	15.00- 18.00
		Coasters for above, ea.	6.00- 7.00
	#7	Water tumbler	7.00- 8.00
	#8	Bowl w/spout (egg beater)	8.00- 9.00
ROW 4:	#1	Drippings dish	25.00- 30.00
		Refrigerator dish	12.00- 14.00
	#2	Flanged lid refrigerator dish, 6"	25.00- 30.00
	#3	Square refrigerator dish	20.00- 25.00
	#4	Sunkist reamer w/o embossing	40.00- 50.00
	#5	Nude "Bottoms Down" mug	85.00-100.00
ROW 5:	#1,2	Canisters, 48 oz. round	20.00- 22.00
	#3	Same, 40 oz.	18.00- 20.00
	#4	Same, 24 oz.	12.00- 15.00
		Same, 10 oz.	10.00- 12.00
	#5	Water bottle	85.00-100.00
ROW 6:	#1-3	Mixing bowl set (4)	35.00- 43.00
		9" (not shown)	12.00- 15.00
		8"	10.00- 12.00
		7"	8.00- 10.00
		6"	5.00- 6.00
	#4	Bowl, 8", flanged rim w/spout	10.00- 12.00
	#5	Cracker bowl, swirl design, hard to find	10.00- 12.00

GREEN TRANSPARENT, HAZEL ATLAS, FEDERAL, JEANNETTE AND OTHERS

There is little room to mention particular items, but I would like to point out pg. 46 Row 3: #4. This reamer is Fenton's "Ming" pattern and is not shown elsewhere in the book. On pg. 47, bottom row, note the shelf holders supporting the third row. They may be only vases, but they work well as shelf supports.

ROW 1:
#1 Canister, glass lid, Hazel Atlas	$30.00-	35.00
#2 Canister, 8 oz., glass lid (rare)	55.00-	65.00
#3 Vinegar jar (8 oz. canister came with this)	18.00-	20.00
#4,5 Embossed Salt or Pepper	22.00-	25.00
#6,7 Embossed Sugar or Flour	30.00-	35.00
#8 Refrigerator dish, 5" x 4½"	12.00-	14.00
#9 Pitcher	10.00-	12.00

ROW 2:
#1-3 REST-WELL mixing bowl set (5)	35.00-	43.00
9½" (not shown)	10.00-	12.00
8½"	8.00-	10.00
7½"	7.00-	8.00
6½"	6.00-	7.00
5½" (shown inside the 6½")	5.00-	6.00
#4 Cruet	25.00-	30.00
#5 Measure cup	14.00-	16.00

ROW 3:
#1-3 Federal mixing bowl set, ribbed, rolled edge (4)	$ 27.00-	32.00

ROW 3 (Continued)
9½" (not shown)	$ 8.00-	10.00
8½"	8.00-	9.00
7½"	6.00-	7.00
6½"	5.00-	6.00
#4 Ruffled edge bowl, 7½"	15.00-	20.00

ROW 4:
#1 Butter dish, 2 lb., Jeannette	90.00-	100.00
#2 Mug	22.50-	25.00
#3 Round salt	100.00-	125.00
#4 Hex Optic ice bucket or reamer bottom	15.00-	17.00

ROW 5:
#1 Floral 4" x 4" refrigerator dish	45.00-	55.00
#2 Hex Optic 4½" x 5" refrigerator dish	15.00-	18.00
#3 Hex Optic butter dish	55.00-	60.00
#4 Measure pitcher, 2 cup	75.00-	85.00
#5 Sugar shaker	40.00-	50.00

Page 46

ROW 1:
#1 Paden City "Party Line" crushed fruit/cookie jar	50.00-	60.00
#2-4 Cambridge set etched #732	175.00-	225.00

ROW 2:
#1 Stack sugar/creamer/plate	40.00-	45.00
#2,3 Marmalade, ea.	20.00-	25.00
#4 Stack set: sugar/creamer/plate/shakers	40.00-	50.00
#5,6 Curtain tie back, ea.	8.00-	10.00
#7 Ash tray	8.00-	10.00

ROW 3:
#1 Cambridge gravy and underliner	45.00-	50.00
#2 Bowl, 7¾"	10.00-	12.50

ROW 3 (Continued)
#3 Toothbrush holder, frosted	12.50-	15.00
#4 Fenton "Ming" reamer	300.00-	350.00
#5 Measure cup, 20 oz.	60.00-	75.00

ROW 4:
#1 Bottom to jar or canister	20.00-	25.00
#2 Kompakt dish units, 8" x 4" (Pat June 16, 1925)	50.00-	65.00
#3 Towel bar	20.00-	25.00
#4,5 Curtain tie backs, pr.	18.00-	20.00
#6-8 Drawer pulls, ea. (large backs $4.00-5.00); small backs	5.00-	7.00
#9 Double drawer pull	18.00-	20.00

Page 47

ROW 1:
#1 "Busy Betty" washing machine	$150.00-	200.00
#2 Barrel cookie jar	40.00-	50.00
#3 4 cup measure pitcher	125.00-	150.00
#4 Single doorknob	20.00-	30.00
#5 Canister embossed COFFEE	75.00-	100.00

ROW 2:
#1 Rolling pin	225.00-	275.00
#2 "Zipper" canister embossed TEA	75.00-	85.00

ROW 3:
#1 Child's washboard embossed CRYSTAL	$150.00-	200.00
#2 Double towel bar	30.00-	35.00
#3 Double doorknob	65.00-	85.00

ROW 4:
#1,5 Store shelf supports, ea.	25.00-	35.00
#2 Pickle jar	75.00-	95.00
#3 Door hook (screw-in type)	17.50-	20.00
#4 Wall coffee dispenser	125.00-	150.00

GREEN TRANSPARENT, U.S. GLASS, TUFGLAS, AND OTHERS

Note the lid on the Fry ice bucket in Row 4: #3 on page 50. This lid suffered a death sentence during an accident at one of our photography sessions. If you have one to sell, please contact me so it can be replaced as soon as possible.

Collectors still have a fascination for the moisture proof shakers shown in the bottom row of page 49. These are mostly found in the South where the humidity is a problem.

Page 51 shows several newly discovered pieces of Tufglas such as the butter dish and funnel. An abundance of jello molds has caused a price adjustment in that particular item for now.

Page 49

ROW 1:

#1	Apothecary jar	$ 20.00-	25.00
#2	Cocktail shaker	55.00-	65.00
#3	Slick-handled 9″ concentric ring bowl w/lid	25.00-	28.00
	w/o lid	15.00-	18.00
#4	Bowl, 9½″, spouted	22.00-	25.00

ROW 2:

#1	Cigarette holder, lid and ash trays	25.00-	28.00
#2	Measure cup	18.00-	20.00
#3	Measure cup, slick handled, 2 spt	25.00-	30.00
#4	Reamer, slick handled	250.00-	300.00

ROW 3:

#1	Refrigerator dish, 6½″ square	22.00-	25.00
#2	Same, 5″ x 9″	22.00-	25.00
#3	Same, 5″ x 5″	10.00-	12.00
#4	Bread box, 6½″ x 10½″	100.00-	110.00

ROW 4:

#1-3	Stack bowl, 9″ w/trivet type lid 9½″	$ 35.00-	40.00
	Stack bowl, 7″ w/trivet type lid 7½″	35.00-	40.00
	Stack bowl, 5″ w /trivet type lid 5½″	28.00-	30.00
	Trivets only, all sizes	12.00-	15.00
#4	Bowl, 9″, 4 footed, sits on plate (muffin dish?)	22.00-	25.00

ROW 5:

#1	Moisture proof shakers (patent 6/25/29) Damp Proof Salt Shaker Co., Inc., Miami	100.00-	125.00
#2	Cake plate	20.00-	22.00
#3,4	Sugar, lid and creamer	22.00-	25.00

Page 50

ROW 1:

#1	Slick handle mixing bowl, 9″ w/9″ lid (w/handles)	$ 35.00-	40.00
#2	Same, only 1 handle	32.00-	35.00
#3	Reamer pitcher, U.S. Glass, 3 pc.	175.00-	225.00

ROW 2:

#1	Slick handle, 7½″ bowl	18.00-	20.00
#2	Refrigerator dish, 4¼″ x 6″, notched holder top	22.00-	25.00
#3	Paden City "Party Line" ice bucket	20.00-	22.00
#4	Same, cruet	40.00-	45.00

ROW 3:

#1	Reamer top shaker, etched pattern (Peacock and Rose)	$150.00-	200.00
	Same, no etching	40.00-	45.00
#2	Ice bucket	22.00-	25.00
#3	Reamer top shaker (called "Speakeasy" by collectors)	30.00-	35.00
#4	Nut dish, metal top	25.00-	30.00
#5	Paden City reamer pitcher	150.00-	200.00

ROW 4:

#1	Cookie jar	30.00-	35.00
#2	Ice bucket	55.00-	60.00
#3	Fry ice bucket, w/lid	175.00-	200.00

TUFGLAS

Page 51

ROW 1:

#1	J.E. Marsden Glassworks mixing bowl, 5 pt., 10″	$ 30.00-	40.00
#2	Same, 3 pt., 9″, made in Ambler, Pa.	25.00-	35.00
#3	Same, 2 pt., 8″, also not for oven use	20.00-	30.00
#4	Same, 1½ pt., 7″, for mixing, cooling and storing food	15.00-	25.00

ROW 2:

#1	Butter dish	55.00-	65.00
#2	Refrigerator dish, 3″ x 6″	20.00-	25.00
#3	Refrigerator dish, 6½″ sq.	30.00-	35.00
#4	"Tufglas Refrigerator Hydrator" No. 1	60.00-	65.00

ROW 3:

#1	Tufglas tab handled spouted bowl	25.00-	30.00
#2	One handled "No Splash Mixer"	30.00-	35.00
#3	Measure pitcher, 36 oz.	50.00-	75.00
#4	Funnel	75.00-	85.00

ROW 3 (Continued)

#5	Custard, "Trade Mark Tufglas Registered"	$ 8.00-	10.00

ROW 4:

#1	Reamer	50.00-	65.00
#2	Bowl, round, 4″	8.00-	10.00
#3	"Kold or Hot" small covered casserole	12.00-	15.00
#4	Jello mold	10.00-	15.00
#5	"Kold or Hot" Sanitary Food Mold	15.00-	18.00

ROW 5:

#1	4 cup "Kold or Hot" measure pitcher	30.00-	35.00
#2	Round refrigerator dish, "To seal, turn cover"	25.00-	30.00
#3	"Sanitary Butter Box", top only	30.00-	35.00
#4	Round bowl, wrinkled ridge, "Kold or Hot"	12.00-	15.00
#5	Custard w/ridges, "Kold or Hot"	2.00-	3.00

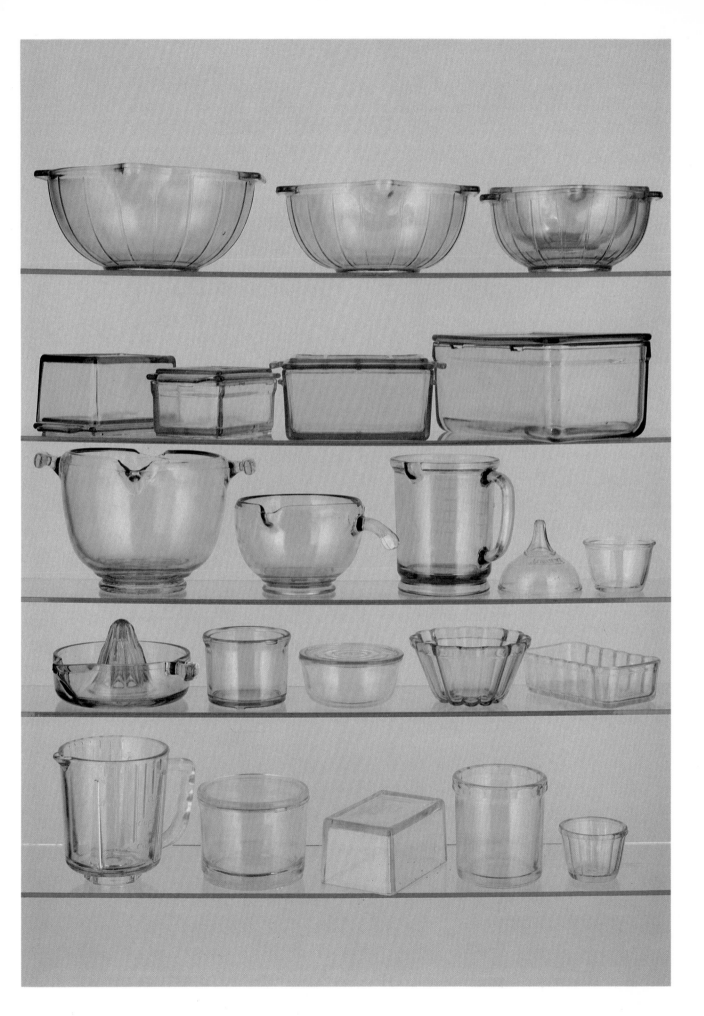

GREEN TRANSPARENT MISCELLANEOUS

The Sneath Company canister set in the top row and the "Zipper" pieces in Row 4 still create a stir among collectors of green. The refrigerator box in Row 5 was incorrectly listed as a bread box last time.

On Row 4: #1 page 54 is a very rare Jenkins reamer pitcher with the lid shown beside it. There is a similar pitcher that the reamer will not fit; so be careful buying pieces separately.

The churn on page 55 is different from the pickle jar shown on page 47. Although they are similar, the churn has a larger opening at the top.

Page 53

ROW 1:
#1-8	Sneath Co. canister set (8)	$300.00-	350.00
	Coffee	90.00-	100.00
	Tea	80.00-	90.00
	Spices, ea.	22.00-	25.00
#9	Salt Box	100.00-	125.00
#10	Cocktail shaker	20.00-	22.00

ROW 2:
#1	Cookie jar	30.00-	35.00
#2	Lattice design water bottle	35.00-	45.00
#3	Lattice design refrigerator jar	12.00-	15.00
#4	McKee ice bucket	20.00-	25.00
#5	McKee grapefruit reamer	250.00-	350.00
#6	Ice tub	16.00-	18.00

ROW 3:
#1	Butter dish	40.00-	50.00
#2	Refrigerator dish (shown w/crystal bottom)	10.00-	12.00
	Same, all green	25.00-	30.00
#3	Bowl, ridged, 10½"	12.00-	15.00
#4	Bowl, ridged, 6"	10.00-	12.00
#5	Shaker	12.00-	15.00

ROW 4:
#1-5	Sneath Mfg. Co. "Quaker" pattern called "Zipper" by collectors		
	Large sugar canister	85.00-	100.00
	Coffee	75.00-	85.00

ROW 4 (Continued)
	Tea (not shown)	$ 55.00-	65.00
	Spices, ea.	18.00-	20.00
#6,7	Mixing bowls, plain, 7¼"	6.00-	7.00
	Same, 9¼" (not shown)	8.00-	10.00
	Same, 8¼" (not shown)	7.00-	8.00
	Same, 6¼" (not shown)	5.00-	6.00
	Same, 5¼" (not shown)	4.00-	5.00

ROW 5:
#1	Refrigerator box w/handles or w/o	45.00-	55.00
#2	Bowl, 7"	15.00-	18.00
#3	Nut dish	4.00-	5.00
#4	Round refrigerator jar w/lid	12.00-	15.00
#5	Round jar w/lid	12.00-	15.00
#6	Milk bottle cap	5.00-	6.00

ROW 6:
#1	Horizontal ribbed bowl, 9¼"	22.00-	25.00
#2,3	Federal mixing bowl set (6)	55.00-	70.00
	11¾" (not shown)	12.00-	15.00
	10¾"	10.00-	12.00
	9¾"	8.00-	10.00
	8¾" (not shown)	8.00-	10.00
	7¾" (not shown)	8.00-	10.00
	6¾" (not shown)	8.00-	10.00
#4	Vidrio beater bottom	12.00-	15.00
	w/beater	15.00-	18.00

Page 54

ROW 1:
#1	Canister, sugar	85.00-	100.00
#2	Cocktail shaker	12.00-	15.00
#3	Ring cocktail shaker	12.00-	15.00
#4	Apothecary jar	25.00-	30.00
#5	Cookie, frosted	40.00-	45.00

ROW 2:
#1	Spouted mixing bowl	15.00-	18.00
#2	Butter tub	22.00-	25.00
#3-5	Three jar set	40.00-	50.00
#6	Mustard	12.00-	15.00
#7	Spouted bowl, 4½"	10.00-	12.50

ROW 3:
#1	Canister, similar to first item in Row 1	25.00-	30.00
#2	Punch ladle	25.00-	35.00
#3	Cambridge fork	25.00-	35.00
#4	Knife rest	12.00-	15.00

ROW 4:
#1	Jenkins reamer pitcher w/lid shown beside it	500.00-	600.00
#3	Canister embossed TEA	25.00-	30.00
#4	Salt	75.00-	85.00
#5	Large salt	100.00-	125.00

Page 55

ROW 1:
#1	Churn	150.00-	200.00
#2	L.E. Smith cookie	60.00-	75.00
#3	Imperial cocktail shaker	25.00-	30.00
#4	Cocktail shaker (Sweet Ad-Aline painted on side)	20.00-	25.00

ROW 2:
#1	Reamer, called "Speakeasy" by collectors	35.00-	40.00
#2	Hocking pinched-in decanter	30.00-	35.00
#3	Cookie jar	30.00-	35.00
#4	Jar	30.00-	35.00
#5	Paden City ftd. tumbler	8.00-	10.00
#6	Glass straw	3.00-	4.00

ROW 3:
#1	Paden City sundae	20.00-	25.50
#2	Covered round dish, 7¼"	25.00-	30.00
#3	Same, 8¼"	30.00-	35.00
#4	Crock, 6¼"	35.00-	40.00

ROW 4:
#1	Tufglas refrigerator dish, 5⅞" sq.	20.00-	25.00
#2	Cold cream jar	8.00-	10.00
#3	Twisted towel bar	20.00-	25.00
#4	Coffee pot lid	2.00-	3.00
#5	Drawer pull	5.00-	7.00

GREEN TRANSPARENT, HOCKING GLASS COMPANY

The "beer and pretzel" set shown on the next page with a 60 oz. pitcher also comes with an 80 oz. pitcher. For now there is a $6.00-9.00 difference in the price. With transparent green on the cover you expect a lot more demand for this particular color as time goes by. Try and find any chalaine blue for sale after it appeared on the cover of the last book!

Page 57

ROW 1:	#1	Decanter, pinched in	$ 28.00-	32.50
	#2	Water bottle	22.00-	25.00
	#3	Water bottle	45.00-	50.00
	#4	Water bottle	20.00-	22.00
	#5	Decanter (same stopper as Cameo)	35.00-	40.00
ROW 2:	#1-6	Pretzel Set (6)	140.00-	160.00
		Pitcher 60 oz.	14.00-	16.00
		Pitcher 80 oz.	20.00-	25.00
		Mug, ea.	20.00-	25.00
		Pretzel jar	50.00-	60.00
ROW 3:	#1,2	Water bottles, 32 oz.	16.00-	18.00
	#3	Same, 62 oz.	18.00-	20.00
	#4,5	Water bottles, raised panels, 32 oz., 2 styles	16.00-	18.00
		Same, 62 oz.	18.00-	20.00

Page 58

ROW 1:	#1-3	Panelled mixing bowl, 11½"	15.00-	18.00
		10¼"	12.00-	15.00
		9½"	10.00-	12.00
ROW 2:	#1,3,4	8½"	10.00-	12.00
		7½"	7.00-	9.00
		6¾"	7.00-	9.00
	#2	8½" bowl, embossed Diamond Crystal Salt	15.00-	18.00
ROW 3:	#1-4	Mixing bowl, 9½"	10.00-	12.00
		8¾"	8.00-	10.00
		7¾"	8.00-	10.00
		6¾"	6.00-	8.00
ROW 4:	#1	Mixing bowl, 10½"	15.00-	18.00
	#2	Batter pitcher	22.00-	25.00
	#3	Batter bowl	20.00-	25.00

Page 59

ROW 1:	#1	Butter dish	15.00-	18.00
	#2	Block Optic butter dish	27.50-	30.00
	#3	Refrigerator dish, Block design	27.00-	30.00
ROW 2:	#1-3	Panelled refrigerator dish, 8" x 8"	20.00-	25.00
		Same, 4" x 8"	12.00-	14.00
		Same, 4" x 4"	10.00-	12.00
ROW 3:	#1	"Vegetable Freshener" embossed on top	65.00-	85.00
	#2,3	Indent handle, 4" x 4", refrigerator dish	12.00-	15.00
		Same, 4" x 8"	14.00-	16.00
ROW 4:	#1-4	Oval refrigerator jars (2 style knobs) 8"	20.00-	22.00
		Same, 7"	18.00-	20.00
		Same, 6"	14.00-	16.00
ROW 5:	#1	Crock, 8"	25.00-	30.00
		Crock, 6½" (not shown)	18.00-	20.00
	#2	Crock, 5"	16.00-	18.00
	#3,4	Round refrigerator jar and cover, 9"	25.00-	30.00
		Same, 7" (not shown)	20.00-	22.00
		Same, 5"	15.00-	18.00

GREEN TRANSPARENT and FIRED-ON COLORS, HOCKING and OTHERS

The Hocking canisters remain the most popular of all those shown in this book. Those with perfect glass lids are difficult to find; the screw-on lids are easier to find, but no less in demand. There is a 4 oz. provision jar to go with the other four in Row 3. I suspect that it is rare because it was never shown in Hocking's catalogues. Besides, what kind of provisions can you store in a 4 oz. jar?

Newly made labels for Hocking or Owens Illinois canisters can be ordered from Lorrie Kitchen, 3905 F Torrance, Toledo, Ohio 43612. Write for price and styles if your labels are missing.

There is little to say about the fired-on colors except there are few collectors and less demand for them than most of the other kitchenware in this book. Of course, that could change!

Page 61

ROW 1:
#1-5 Canisters, 47 oz. w/glass lid	$35.00-	40.00
#6-8 Shakers, ea.	8.00-	10.00

ROW 2:
#1 Canister, screw-on lid, 64 oz.	30.00-	35.00
#2,3 Same, 40 oz.	25.00-	30.00
#4 Same, 20 oz.	20.00-	22.50
#5 Shaker, 8 oz., labeled "Domino Sugar"	12.00-	15.00
#6,7 Shakers, ea.	8.00-	10.00

ROW 3:
#1-4 Provision jars, 64 oz.	25.00-	30.00
Same, 32 oz.	20.00-	22.00
Same, 16 oz.	12.00-	15.00

ROW 3 (Continued)
Same, 8 oz.	$10.00-	12.00
Same, 4 oz. (not shown)	40.00-	50.00
#5,7 Round shakers, pr.	30.00-	35.00
#6 Drip jar	18.00-	20.00

ROW 4:
#1 Canister	25.00-	30.00
#2-5 Smooth sided canister, 40 oz., screw-on lid	22.00-	25.00
Same, 20 oz.	18.00-	20.00
Same, 8 oz., ea.	8.00-	10.00
#6,7 Shakers, pr. (sold individually as sugar shakers)	25.00-	35.00
#8,9 Milk bottle caps, ea.	4.00-	5.00

Page 62

ROW 1:
#1 Cocktail shaker	$15.00-	18.00
#2 Cocktail shaker (pinched-in sides)	28.00-	30.00
#3 Onion chopper	10.00-	12.00
#4 Cigarette jar, ash tray on top	14.00-	16.00
#5 Toothpick	8.00-	10.00
#6 Electric beater	18.00-	20.00

ROW 2:
#1 Measure cup	45.00-	50.00
#2-4 Measure cups, ea.	15.00-	18.00
#5 Syrup	18.00-	20.00
#6 Cruet	22.00-	25.00
#7 Ash tray	8.00-	10.00

ROW 3:
#1 2-piece reamer	$22.00-	25.00
#2 Reamer pitcher	15.00-	18.00
#3 2-piece reamer ribbed pitcher	45.00-	50.00
#4 2-piece reamer	18.00-	22.00

ROW 4:
#1 Reamer, odd shade	15.00-	20.00
#2 "Coke" bottle green	15.00-	18.00
#3 Reamer, shade most collected	12.00-	15.00
#4 Tab handled reamer	10.00-	12.00
#5 Tab handled reamer	8.00-	10.00

Page 63

ROW 1:
#1 Canister, yellow	$12.00-	15.00
#2 Canister, ribbed green	10.00-	12.00
Canister, small	6.00-	7.00
#3 Shaker	4.00-	5.00
#4 Hazel Atlas coffee	20.00-	22.00
#5 Same, Tea	15.00-	18.00
#6 Hocking tea canister	12.00-	15.00

ROW 2:
#1 Milk pitcher, 16 oz.	5.00-	6.00
#2,3 Same, cream, 8 oz.	4.00-	5.00
#4 Syrup	6.00-	8.00
#5 Gemco shaker (not too old)	8.00-	10.00
#6 Shaker, Hocking	4.00-	6.00

ROW 3:
#1-3 Hocking refrigerator dish, 5½" x 4¾"	3.00-	4.00
Same, 9" x 5¼"	4.00-	5.00
#4 Water bottle w/clear lid	6.00-	8.00

ROW 4:
#1-3 Round refrig. bowl, 5½", ea.	3.00-	4.00
#4 Pitcher, 20 oz.	4.00-	5.00

ROW 5:
#1-3 Dutch shakers, ea. (set/4: also green boy)	5.00-	6.00
#4,5 Tappan shakers, pr.	7.00-	8.00
#6,7 Shakers, McKee, ea.	7.00-	8.00
#8 "Crisscross" design bowl, 5¼"	5.00-	6.00

PINK

Pink kitchenware is harder to find than the green. For a while there were many collectors looking for the pink, but some of those have turned to other colors or other items in this realm. On the next page are some of the newer items that have appeared since the last book.

The large covered jar in the top row belongs to Paden City's "Party Line". The catalogue lists this as "Hi Crushed Fruit Bowl and Cover", but most collectors today consider it a cookie jar. The rest of that row contains a Jenkins batter jug and a Cambridge counterpart. There is a smaller syrup to go with the latter, but I am not so sure about the Jenkins batter.

Row 2 shows a dispenser of some sort. It is believed to be a sugar by its owner, but there are some interesting speculations beyond that. A blue one shown earlier (page 17) is marked "Monroe Mfg. Co., Elgin Ill., Pat Pend." If anyone out there knows of this company or their products, please contact me.

The next two items are U.S. Glass. The first is a "Paramount" napkin holder and the other is a "Shari" cosmetic holder. The top lifts off to reveal places for lipsticks and other "make-over" equipment.

In Row 3 resides a Fenton "Ming" reamer and a Tufglas jello mold. Whereas the green mold is very common, the pink is not.

The middle measuring cup in Row 4 is Cambridge. This is collectible in several areas of kitchenware as well as by collectors of Cambridge glass. Items that reach across several fields of collecting are always in demand and worthwhile to own.

ROW 1:	#1	Paden City "Party Line" crushed fruit/cookie jar	$40.00- 50.00
	#2	Jenkins batter pitcher	75.00- 90.00
	#3	Cambridge batter jug for waffle set	60.00- 70.00
	#4	Cocktail shaker	60.00- 65.00
ROW 2:	#1	Dispenser (possibly sugar)	150.00-200.00
	#2	Paramount napkin holder (U.S. Glass)	175.00-200.00
	#3	U.S. Glass "SHARI" cosmetic holder (2 pc.)	100.00-125.00
	#4	Stack set: sugar/creamer/plate/shakers	40.00- 50.00
ROW 3:	#1	Cambridge double gravy boat	22.00- 25.00
	#2	Imperial gravy boat	18.00- 20.00
	#3	Fenton "Ming" 2-piece reamer	300.00-400.00
	#4	Tufglas jello mold	22.00- 25.00
ROW 4:	#1	Paden City Party Line ice tub	22.00- 25.00
	#2	U.S. Glass 2 cup measure	125.00-150.00
	#3	Cambridge 1 cup measure	150.00-200.00
	#4	Stack sugar/creamer/lid	30.00- 35.00
	#5,6	Curtain tie backs, ea.	8.00- 10.00
ROW 5:	#1,2	Curtain tie backs, ea.	11.00- 14.00
	#3	Drawer pull, single	5.00- 6.00
	#4,5	Single towel rods, 18″, ea.	22.00- 25.00
	#6	Double towel rod	25.00- 28.00

PINK Continued

The pretzel jar shown in the top row has no mugs but a pitcher to go with it just as the green one shown on page 57. Actually the pink is harder to find, but there are more collectors of the green set which makes the price higher. As in any collectible, demand for an item determines price more than rarity. A piece can be one of a kind, but if no one wishes to buy it then it will not bring a high price. I started to say that it will not have a high price, but there are some who would price it high whether anyone was interested in buying it or not.

The Hazel Atlas embossed shakers in Row 5 are hard to find in pink. Pink *flour* and *sugar* are even harder to find than the green ones!

HOCKING GLASS COMPANY

ROW 1:	#1	Pretzel jar	$ 35.00- 40.00
	#2-4	Canisters, plain, 40 oz.	35.00- 40.00
		20 oz. (not shown)	30.00- 35.00
		8 oz.	25.00- 30.00
	#5	Refrigerator dish, 4″ x 4″, indented handles	10.00- 12.50
	#6	Measure pitcher, 2 cup, ribbed	25.00- 30.00

FEDERAL GLASS COMPANY

ROW 2:	#1-4	Mixing bowl set (4)	35.00- 45.00
		9½″	12.00- 15.00
		8½″	10.00- 12.00
		7½″	8.00- 10.00
		6½″	6.00- 7.00
ROW 3:	#1,2,4	Refrigerator dish set (3)	45.00- 55.00
		8″ x 8″	25.00- 30.00
		4″ x 8″	15.00- 18.00
		4″ x 4″	6.00- 8.00
	#3	Refrigerator dish, 3¾″ x 5¾″, w/legs	8.00- 10.00
	#5	Butter dish, ¼ lb.	20.00- 25.00
ROW 4:	#1	Butter dish, 1 lb.	35.00- 40.00
	#2	4″ x 4″ vegetable embossed lid (asparagus)	15.00- 18.00
		4″ x 8″ vegetable embossed lid (not shown)	20.00 25.00
	#3,4	Round refrigerator dish, 4½″	12.00- 15.00
		Same, 5½″	10.00- 12.00
	#5	Reamer, Federal	85.00-100.00

HAZEL ATLAS GLASS COMPANY

ROW 5:	#1,2	Mixing bowls, 11⅝″ (not shown)	18.00- 20.00
		10⅝″ (not shown)	15.00- 18.00
		9⅝″	10.00- 12.00
		8½″ (not shown)	10.00- 12.00
		7⅝″	8.00- 10.00
		6⅝″ (not shown)	6.00- 8.00
	#3,4	Salt or pepper, embossed	25.00- 35.00
	#5	Cruet	35.00- 40.00
	#6	Milk pitcher	15.00- 20.00
ROW 6:	#1-4	REST-WELL mixing bowl set (5)	40.00- 50.00
		9½″	12.00- 15.00
		8½″	10.00- 12.00
		7½″	8.00- 10.00
		6½″ (not shown)	6.00- 8.00
		5½″	5.00- 6.00

PINK Continued

Many of the items shown on this page are U.S. Glass Company, but there are other companies represented too. The slick handles made by them are rather distinctive and hard to miss. There is an abundance of slick handled bowls around, but the covers for these bowls are a different matter. I know these bowls are heavy and that has probably accounted for their longevity since they are awkward to handle when pouring the contents, holding on to that protrusion. The ones with two handles are a little better, but the one-handled ones are difficult at best.

ROW 1:	#1	Utility pitcher	$30.00- 35.00
	#2	Slick handle measure pitcher	27.00- 30.00
	#3	Measure cup	40.00- 45.00
	#4	Cruet	40.00- 45.00
	#5	Cruet	32.00- 35.00
	#6	Apothecary jar	20.00- 22.00
ROW 2:	#1	Heisey cigarette and ash tray	50.00- 60.00
	#2	Cruet set	80.00- 95.00
	#3	Mixing bowl, 7″	12.00- 14.00
		Same, 5″	8.00- 10.00
		Same, 9″	15.00- 18.00
	#4	Mug, "Adams Rib"	12.00- 15.00
	#5	Ice pail	15.00- 18.00
ROW 3:	#1	Round crock, 8″, lid fits outside	25.00- 30.00
	#2	Same, 6½″	20.00- 25.00
	#3	Round refrigerator dish, tab handle	22.00- 25.00
	#4	"Kompakt" dish unit	30.00- 35.00
ROW 4:	#1	Slick handle mixing bowl, 8¾″ w/lid, spouted	30.00- 35.00
		Same w/o lid	10.00- 15.00
	#2	Slick handle mixing bowl, 9″, (2 handles, spouted)	22.00- 25.00
		Same w/lid	35.00- 38.00
	#3	Slick handle bowl, 7½″, spouted, "D&B" embossed	18.00- 20.00
ROW 5:	#1	Slick handle 9″ concentric ring bowl	20.00- 22.00
		Same, w/lid	32.00- 35.00
	#2	Snowflake cake plate	15.00- 20.00
	#3	2 handle bowl, no spout, 9″	18.00- 20.00

PINK Continued

There is really a wide variety of pink shown here. Most notable in Row 3 are the moisture proof shakers. In Row 4 is the complete "Tricia" reamer and the base to a dispenser shown completed on page 65.

ROW 1:	#1	Hex Optic stack set, Jeannette; base ($12.00-15.00); lid ($8.00-10.00)	$ 45.00- 55.00
	#2	Hex Optic flat rim mixing bowl, 9″	20.00- 22.00
		Same, 10″ (not shown)	22.00- 25.00
		Same, 8¼″ (not shown)	16.00- 18.00
		Same, 7¼″ (not shown)	12.00- 15.00
	#3	Hex Optic ruffled edge mixing bowl, 8¼″	18.00- 20.00
		Same, 10½″ (not shown)	22.00- 25.00
		Same, 6″ (not shown)	15.00- 17.00
	#4	Ice bucket w/lid, Fry	60.00- 75.00
ROW 2:	#1	Butter box, 2 lb. embossed "B," Jeannette	90.00-110.00
	#2	Round salt	75.00- 85.00
	#3,4	Flat Jennyware shakers, pr.	50.00- 55.00
	#5	Tumbler	8.00- 10.00
	#6	Cruet	40.00- 45.00
	#7	Barber bottle	12.00- 15.00
ROW 3:	#1,2	Moisture proof shakers, pr.	110.00-125.00
	#3	Reamer, probably foreign	40.00- 45.00
		Same, sun colored amethyst (not shown)	35.00- 45.00
		Same, crystal (not shown)	20.00- 25.00
	#4	Tumbler, imprinted Mission Juice	20.00- 25.00
	#5,6	Quilted refrigerator jars, w/lid 8 oz.	15.00- 20.00
		4 oz.	12.00- 15.00
	#7	Stack sugar, creamer and lid	30.00- 32.00
	#8	Same only with place for salt and pepper	30.00- 35.00
		Salt and pepper on above	40.00- 50.00
ROW 4:	#1	MacBeth Evans stack set	40.00- 50.00
	#2	Ice bucket	18.00- 20.00
	#3	Ice bucket w/Sterling bear	35.00- 40.00
	#4	Reamer called "Tricia" by collectors	400.00-450.00
	#5	Dispenser w/insert (insert not shown)	150.00-200.00
ROW 5:	#1	Reamer, grapefruit	135.00-160.00
	#2	Paden City syrup Jug	22.00- 25.00
	#3	New Martinsville syrup jug	25.00- 30.00
	#4,5	Heisey Twist cruet, 2½ oz.	60.00- 70.00
		4 oz.	65.00- 75.00
	#6	Heisey Twist mustard w/spoon	60.00- 70.00
		w/o spoon	40.00- 50.00
	#7	Cambridge syrup	45.00- 55.00
ROW 6:	#1	Bowl, 9¾″ marked Cambridge	20.00- 22.00
	#2	Bowl, 7¾″ plain bottom	8.00- 10.00
	#3	Bowl, 8″, concentric rings in bottom	10.00- 12.00
	#4	Butter dish, bow handled top	40.00- 45.00

RED, TRANSPARENT and FIRED-ON

The cocktail shaker boot is quite astounding, but then, so is the Silex coffee pot next to it. I have trouble visualizing a red kitchen, but there are some highly unusual pieces to be found in this color. The fired-on red on page 75 affects collectors in one of two ways. They either hate it or love it. There does not seem to be any middle ground.

Page 73

ROW 1:

#1 Boot cocktail shaker	$100.00-150.00
#2 Silex coffee pot	100.00-125.00
#3 Decanter w/shot glass stopper	50.00- 65.00

ROW 2:

#1 Cocktail shaker	25.00- 30.00
#2 3 oz. tumbler that goes w/#1	2.00- 3.00

ROW 2 (Continued)

#3 Barbell cocktail shaker (possibly New Martinsville)	$ 60.00- 75.00
#4 Duncan Miller cocktail shaker	35.00- 45.00
#5 Cocktail shaker	25.00- 35.00

ROW 3:

#1 McKee batter pitcher	65.00- 80.00
#2 Batter pitcher w/tray	85.00-100.00
#3,4 Tumble-up set	100.00-125.00

Page 74

ROW 1:

#1 Hocking tumbler w/Old Reliable tea bags	$ 10.00- 12.00
#2,3 Hocking water bottles, plain or ribbed	40.00- 50.00
#4 Food chopper	20.00- 25.00
#5 Strawholder (possibly 60's)	150.00-200.00
#6 Hocking 24 oz. beater jar	35.00- 40.00

ROW 2:

#1 Cambridge "Mt. Vernon" ice bucket	75.00- 85.00
#2 Hocking ice bucket	30.00- 35.00
#3 Cruet	75.00- 95.00
#4 Sugar shaker (possibly 60's)	45.00- 60.00
#5,6 Wheaton Nuline shakers, pr.	35.00- 40.00
#7,8 Hocking shakers (possibly 60's), pr.	25.00- 35.00

ROW 3:

#1 Imperial gravy and platter	125.00-150.00
#2 Butter w/crystal top	50.00- 65.00

ROW 3 (Continued)

#3-5 Mixing bowl set (3)	$100.00-125.00
9¼"	45.00- 50.00
7¾"	30.00- 40.00
6½"	25.00- 35.00

ROW 4:

#1 Tea pot top	12.00- 15.00
#2 Knob escutcheon plate for door knob	10.00- 12.00
#3 Double drawer pull	35.00- 45.00
#4 Single drawer pull	20.00- 25.00
#5,6 Curtain rings, ea.	10.00- 12.00
#7,8 Feathered curtain tie backs, pr.	25.00- 35.00

ROW 5:

#1 Trivet	40.00- 50.00
#2 Tray (possibly for a New Martinsville set)	50.00- 65.00
#3,4 Fork and spoon set	85.00-100.00

Page 75

ROW 1:

#1 Salt canister, press-on lid	$ 20.00- 25.00
#2,3 Shakers, ea.	4.00- 5.00
#4-6 Hocking canisters, 40 oz.	12.00- 15.00
Same, 20 oz.	10.00- 12.00
Shakers, 8 oz., ea.	8.00- 10.00

ROW 2:

#1,2 Hocking ribbed canisters, 47 oz., glass lid	18.00- 20.00
#3,4 Shakers, ea.	3.00- 4.00
#5 Drip jar	10.00- 15.00
#6 Water bottle	8.00- 10.00
#7 Tappan shaker	7.00- 8.00

ROW 3:

#1-4 Owens-Illinois canisters (ovoid shape) Coffee	20.00- 22.00

ROW 3 (Continued)

Tea	$ 15.00- 18.00
Shakers, ea.	6.00- 7.00
#5 MacBeth Evans canister, "Gold Medal Flour"	10.00- 12.00
#6 Sugar shaker (Gemco)	12.00- 15.00

ROW 4:

#1 McKee water bottle (tumbler makes top)	12.00- 15.00
#2 McKee water bottle, stopper	18.00- 20.00
#3-5 Hocking canister set (late)	18.00- 20.00

ROW 5:

#1 Hocking 10½" mixing bowl	7.00- 8.00
#2 Vitrock 6¾" bowl	6.00- 8.00
#3 Federal 5" bowl	2.00- 3.00

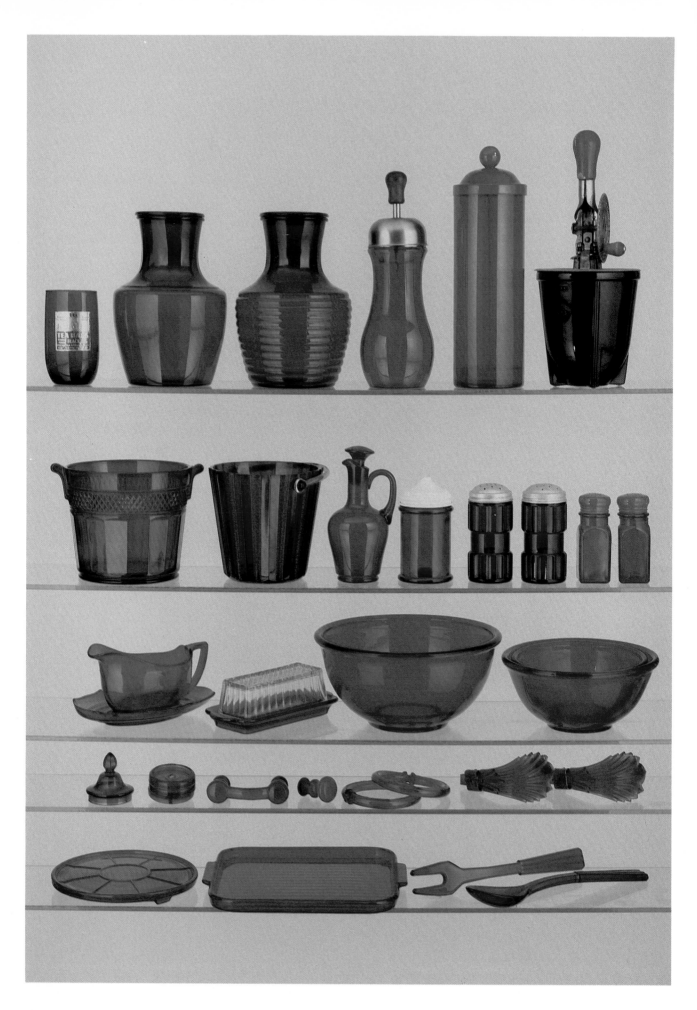

WHITE

There have not been any great price adjustments in white since the last book, but there have been quite a few collectors getting on its bandwagon. There are two major reasons for this, availability and price. Those are two major concerns of new collectors. Can I find it and can I afford it? This meets the criteria well. The trimmed in red or green items are more in demand than the non-trimmed ones.

Page 77 (HAZEL ATLAS)

ROW 1:	#1	Butter dish, Fairmont's Better "Patty Roll" Butter	$ 25.00-	30.00
	#2	Same, Fairmont's Better Butter	30.00-	35.00
	#3	Decorated butter dish	55.00-	65.00
	#4	Refrigerator dish, 6" round	15.00-	18.00
	#5	Beater Bowl	8.00-	10.00
ROW 2:	#1	Bowl, 8"	6.00-	8.00
	#2,3	Pitcher, reamer or beater top	28.00-	32.50
	#4	Measure pitcher, 4 cup	18.00-	20.00
ROW 3:	#1,2	Mixing bowl, 8¾"	6.00-	7.00
		6¾"	4.00-	5.00
	#3	Refrigerator dish, 6"	18.00-	20.00
	#4	Milk pitcher	10.00-	12.00
	#5	Reamer, 2 piece	25.00-	30.00
ROW 4:	#1-4	Mixing bowl set (4)	15.00-	20.00
		8"	6.00-	7.00
		7"	4.00-	5.00
		6"	3.00-	4.00
		5"	3.00-	4.00
ROW 5:	#1	Bowl, Crisscross, 6¾"	3.00-	4.00
	#2	Bowl, 5¼", straight edge	3.00-	4.00
	#3	Refrigerator dish, 4½" x 5", will not stack	10.00-	12.00
	#4,5	Shakers, ea.	5.00-	6.00
	#6	Tumbler, 4", 8 oz.	4.00-	5.00

Page 78

ROW 1:	#1-4	Shakers, ea.	5.00-	6.00
	#5,6	Shakers, marked Electrochef, ea.	6.00-	8.00
	#7	Shaker, marked Home Soap Company	12.00-	15.00
	#8	Spice set in original box	12.00-	15.00
ROW 2:	#1,2	Shakers, labelled Frank Tea & Spice Co., pr.	8.00-	9.00
	#3	Napkin holder, "Fort Howard Handi-Nap Napkins"	25.00-	30.00
	#4	Same, "Nar-O-Fold"	20.00-	25.00
	#5	Refrigerator jar, "Breakstone's Fine Dairy Foods"	8.00-	10.00
	#6	Androck whipper	10.00-	15.00
ROW 3:	#1	U.S. Glass reamer, 2 piece	100.00-	125.00
	#2	Reamer, Fleur w/rib	70.00-	85.00
	#3	Reamer, U.S. Glass	20.00-	25.00
	#4	Reamer	20.00-	25.00
ROW 4:	#1	Pickle ladle	12.00-	15.00
	#2	Welch-Ade dispenser	100.00-	125.00
	#3	Pitcher	20.00-	25.00
	#4	Salt box	70.00-	80.00

Page 79 (McKEE GLASS COMPANY)

ROW 1:	#1-4	Canisters, 48 oz., screw-on lid, ea.	30.00-	35.00
	#5,6	Shakers, ea.	25.00-	30.00
ROW 2:	#1-4	Shakers, ea.	5.00-	6.00
	#5	Butter churn	25.00-	30.00
	#6,8	Shakers, Roman arch side panels, ea.	6.00-	8.00
	#7	Sugar, same	25.00-	28.00
ROW 3:	#1	Round Canister, 32 oz. (red letters)	20.00-	25.00
	#2	Refrigerator water dispenser	85.00-	100.00
	#3	Round canister, 32 oz. (black letters)	16.00-	18.00
ROW 4:	#1	Teapot, Glasbake	40.00-	45.00
	#2	Teapot, w/lid	22.00-	25.00
	#3	Coffee server	55.00-	60.00
	#4	Individual coffee server	3.00-	4.00
	#5	Salt shaker, "Diamond Check"	12.50-	15.00

YELLOW, OPAQUE and TRANSPARENT, McKEE, HOCKING and OTHERS

On page 82, Hocking's measure pitcher in Row 3, large canisters in Row 4, and the batter pitcher in Row 6 are all experimental pieces. It is doubtful you will find others in case you have been looking. The transparent yellow on page 83 has several items of note. In the top row is a U.S. Glass pitcher reamer set and in the next row is a sugar shaker.

McKEE GLASS COMPANY
Page 81
ROW 1:
#1 Canister, 48 oz., screw-on lid	$45.00-	55.00
#2-4 Canister, 48 oz., press-on lid	45.00-	55.00
#5-8 Shakers, 8 oz., ea.	8.00-	10.00

ROW 2:
#1,2 Round canister, 48 oz., w/lid	27.00-	30.00
#3 Same, 40 oz.	25.00-	27.00
#4 Same, 24 oz.	18.00-	20.00
Same, 10 oz. (not shown)	15.00-	17.00
#5 Measuring cup, 2 spout	150.00-	200.00

ROW 3:
#1-3 Mixing bowl set (3)	50.00-	60.00
9″	20.00-	22.50
7½″	18.00-	20.00
6″	12.00-	15.00
#4 Pitcher, 2 cup measure	45.00-	55.00

ROW 4:
#1 Bowl, ribbed "Manning Bowman," 9½″	$ 12.00-	15.00
#2 Bowl, ribbed, 6½″	8.00-	10.00
#3 Bowl, "Hamilton Beach," 9¼″	10.00-	12.00
#4 "Bottoms Down" mug	115.00-	130.00

ROW 5:
#1 Mixing bowl, 7″, part of set	18.00-	20.00
Same, 9″ (not shown)	22.00-	25.00
Same, 8″ (not shown)	18.00-	20.00
Same, 6″ (not shown)	15.00-	18.00
#2 Bowl, 7″ w/spout	14.00-	16.00
#3 Bowl, 4½″	8.00-	10.00
#4 Pitcher, 2 cup measure	30.00-	35.00

McKee's Seville Yellow
Page 82
ROW 1:
#1 Butter dish	$ 55.00	65.00
#2,3 Refrigerator dish, flanged lid, 7″	40.00-	45.00
Same, 6″	35.00-	40.00
#4 Sunkist reamer	40.00-	45.00

ROW 2:
#1 Refrigerator tray, 8¼″ x 12½″	28.00-	30.00
#2 Stack refrigerator dish, 4″ x 5″	10.00-	12.00
Same, 8″ x 5″	18.00-	22.00
#3 Salt bowl	80.00-	90.00

ROW 3:
#1 Drip jar	30.00-	35.00
#2 Rolling pin	175.00-	200.00

ROW 3 (Continued)
#3 Measure pitcher (Hocking), experimental	$175.00-	200.00

HOCKING GLASS COMPANY
ROW 4:
#1-3 Canister, 40 oz., experimental	55.00-	65.00
#4,5 Canister, 20 oz. (black letters)	20.00-	22.00
Same (red letters)	22.00-	24.00
#6-8 Shakers, ea.	9.00-	11.00
#9 Refrigerator jar, 4″ x 4″	5.00-	8.00

ROW 5:
#1 Batter pitcher, experimental	50.00-	60.00
#2,3 Refrigerator dish, 8″ x 8″	40.00-	50.00
Same, 4″ x 4″	30.00-	40.00

Yellow Transparent
Page 83
ROW 1:
#1 Fenton ice bucket	$ 75.00-	85.00
#2 U.S. Glass reamer pitcher	400.00-	500.00
#3 Glass for above set	12.00-	15.00
#4 Fostoria ice bucket	30.00-	40.00
#5 Fostoria oil and vinegar	75.00-	85.00
#6 Fostoria "Mayfair" cruet	60.00-	75.00

ROW 2:
#1 Fostoria oil and vinegar	45.00-	50.00
#2 Fostoria "Mayfair" syrup and liner	50.00-	65.00
#3 Sugar shaker	150.00-	175.00
#4 Hazel Atlas 2 cup reamer set	200.00-	250.00
#5 Hazel Atlas mug	25.00-	35.00
#6 Duncan "Festive" gravy and ladle	30.00-	40.00

ROW 3:
#1 Heisey syrup	60.00-	75.00
#2 Heisey "Old Sandwich" cruet w/stopper	65.00-	75.00
#3 Hazel Atlas 1 cup measure, 3 spout	175.00-	225.00

ROW 3 (Continued)
#4 Hazel Atlas egg cup	$ 3.00-	5.00
#5 Canning funnel "C.W. Hart", Troy, N.Y.	35.00-	50.00
#6 Hazel Atlas refrigerator dish 4½″ x 5″	20.00-	25.00

ROW 4:
#1 Hazel Atlas REST-WELL mixing bowl, 8¾″	22.00-	25.00
#2 Same, 7¾″	20.00-	22.00
#3 Same, 6¾″	16.00-	18.00
#4 Same, 5¾″	12.00-	15.00

ROW 5:
#1 U.S. Glass slick handled batter bowl	30.00-	35.00
#2 Soap dish	18.00-	20.00
#3 Heisey sugar cube tray	60.00-	75.00
#4 Spoon, salad size	20.00-	25.00
#5 Spoon, regular size	25.00-	30.00

PART 2 KITCHEN ITEMS
BATTER JUGS and BUTTER DISHES

Batter jugs come in a multitude of colors and make a nice display if you have the room to show them. Of course, the cobalt blues are the most popular, but the lid to the Jeannette Jadite is the hardest piece to find of them all. Many collectors started with butter dishes as they originally did in the collecting of Depression glass. That trend seems to have faded.

Page 85

ROW 1:
#1 Paden City crystal w/black lids set	$ 85.00-100.00	
#2 Paden City black set	160.00-185.00	
#3 Paden City pink w/black tray set	100.00-125.00	

ROW 2:
#1 Paden City batter jug	40.00- 45.00	
#2 Paden City milk jug	35.00- 40.00	
#3 Paden City syrup	30.00- 35.00	
#4 Paden City green batter jug	35.00- 40.00	
#5 Cambridge pink batter jug for waffle set	60.00- 70.00	
#6 Cambridge amber syrup jug	40.00- 50.00	

ROW 3:
#1 Jenkins #570 green batter jug	$ 65.00- 80.00	
#2 Green batter jug	35.00- 45.00	
#3 Square green batter jug	45.00- 55.00	
#4 Jenkins green batter jug	400.00-500.00	

ROW 4:
#1 Jenkins pink batter jug	75.00- 90.00	
#2 Jeannette Jadite (bottom only-45.00-50.00)	125.00-150.00	
#3 Liberty "American Pioneer" batter jug	150.00-165.00	
#4 Same, syrup jug	125.00-140.00	

Page 86

ROW 1:
#1 New Martinsville cobalt blue batter set	$225.00-250.00	
#2 Same, amber	85.00-110.00	
#3 Red batter jug and liner	85.00-100.00	

ROW 2:
#1 New Martinsville green batter jug	40.00- 50.00	
#2 Same, syrup jug	30.00- 40.00	

ROW 2 (Continued)
#3 New Martinsville crystal batter w/green top	$ 25.00- 30.00	
#4 New Martinsville pink syrup jug	25.00- 30.00	

ROW 3
#1 McKee black batter	50.00- 60.00	
#2 Same, white	55.00- 60.00	
#3 Same, blue	65.00- 80.00	
#4 Same, red	65.00- 80.00	

Page 87

ROW 1:
#1 Embossed "Islay", amber	$ 40.00- 50.00	
#2 Pink tub	12.00- 15.00	
#3 White, butter or cheese, w/slicer	60.00- 75.00	
#4 Amber tub	20.00- 22.50	
#5 Green, ribbed	18.00- 22.00	

ROW 2:
#1 Skokie green, McKee	30.00- 35.00	
#2 Custard, McKee	30.00- 35.00	
#3 Crystal, embossed "Butter"	18.00- 20.00	

ROW 3:
#1 Custard w/green trim, McKee	35.00- 45.00	
#2 "Ships", McKee	18.00- 20.00	
#3 White w/flower decal, McKee	18.00- 20.00	

ROW 4:
#1 Pink, Federal, 1 lb.	35.00- 40.00	
#2 Amber, Federal, ¼ lb.	22.00- 25.00	
#3 Amber, Federal, ¼ lb.	22.00- 25.00	

ROW 4 (Continued)
#4 Green	$ 30.00- 35.00	
Pink	35.00- 40.00	

ROW 5:
#1 White w/red, Hazel Atlas, "Fairmont's"	30.00- 35.00	
#2 Frosted green, "Crisscross", Hazel Atlas, ¼ lb.	20.00- 22.00	
#3 Blue, "Crisscross", Hazel Atlas, 1 lb.	55.00- 65.00	
#4 White w/red, Hazel Atlas, "Fairmont's", round	25.00- 30.00	

ROW 6:
#1 Delphite, Jeannette	85.00-100.00	
#2 Pink, "Jennyware", Jeannette	60.00- 65.00	
#3 Pink, butter box, Jeannette, 2 lb., embossed "B"	90.00-110.00	
#4 Green, Jeannette bottom, metal cover	15.00- 18.00	

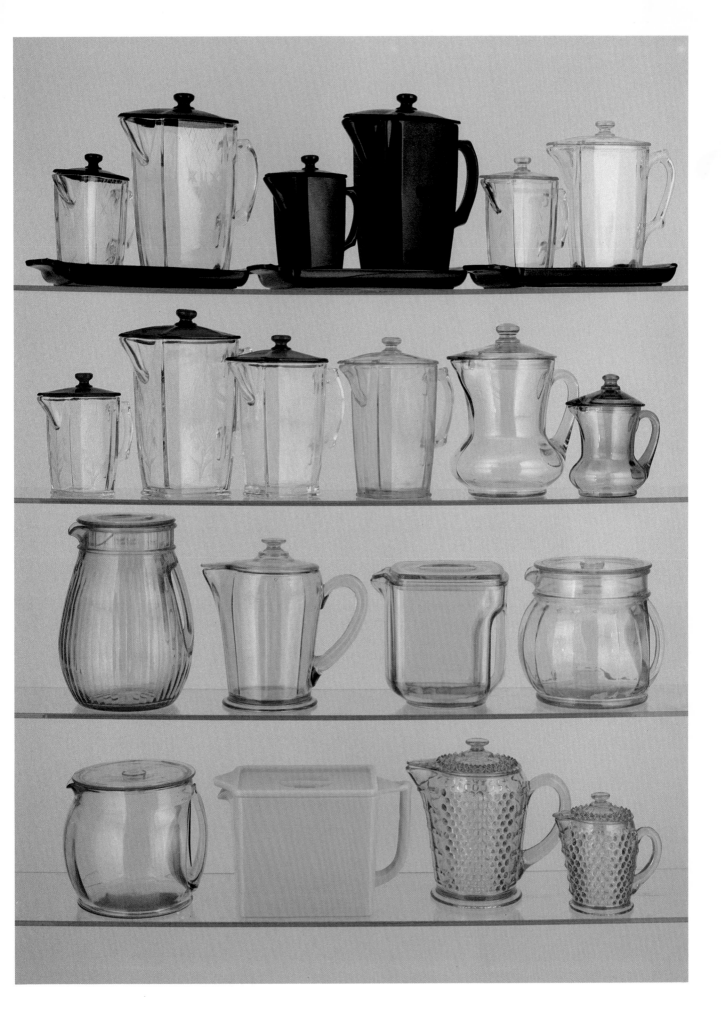

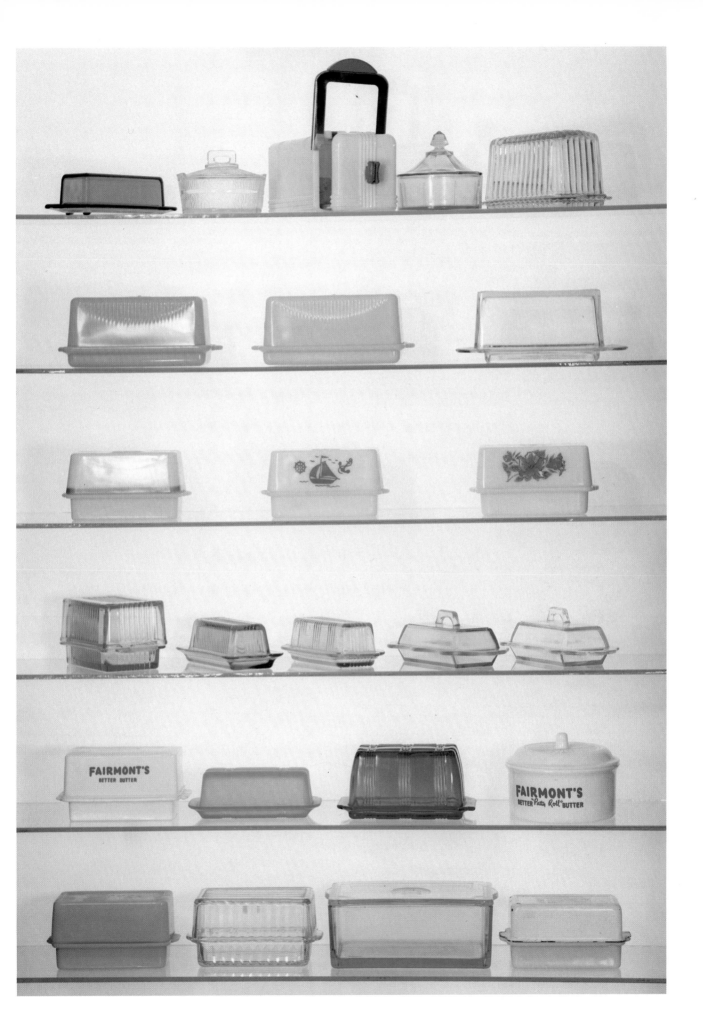

BUTTER DISHES and CHEESE DISHES

The price on those dotted butters has really risen since the last book. I warned you they were hard to find!

Unfortunately, the brownish background takes away from some of the represented colors, but pay particular attention to the design differences on the McKee butters in Row 4. The Seville yellow has tabbed handles and ridges while the Chalaine blue is plain with no ridges. The Chalaine comes in both styles and you can see each on page 15.

The reproductions of the cheese preserver has stiffled the prices on those for the present. The lid for the preserver gives instructions to "Lift the lid daily-Let air circulate" and to "Place a fourth pint of vinegar and a half tablespoon of salt in the bottom, dilute slightly with water".

ROW 1:	#1	¼ lb. red bottom, crystal top	$ 50.00- 65.00
	#2	¼ lb. frosted crystal	12.00- 15.00
	#3	¼ lb. Federal pink	20.00- 25.00
	#4	¼ lb. Heisey crystal	50.00- 60.00
	#5	¼ lb. Hazel Atlas Platonite	12.00- 14.00
	#6	¼ lb. Hocking Fire King Jad-ite bottom, crystal top	8.00- 10.00
ROW 2	#1	1 lb. green	40.00- 50.00
	#2	1 lb. Jennyware ultra-marine	150.00-175.00
	#3	1 lb. green Clambroth	40.00- 50.00
	#4	1 lb. restaurant ware green	35.00- 40.00
ROW 3:	#1	1 lb. Hazel Atlas black Dots	40.00- 45.00
	#2	1 lb. Hazel Atlas pink	50.00- 55.00
	#3	1 lb. Hazel Atlas cobalt blue	125.00-150.00
	#4	1 lb. Jeannette Hex Optic green	55.00- 60.00
	#5	1 lb. Jeannette Jadite green	35.00- 40.00
ROW 4:	#1	1 lb. McKee Seville yellow	55.00- 65.00
	#2	1 lb. McKee Chalaine blue, plain, no tabs	225.00-250.00
	#3	1 lb. crystal embossed "Butter"	18.00- 20.00
	#4	1 lb. crystal embossed "Louella-finest butter in America"	20.00- 22.00
ROW 5:	#1	1 lb. McKee Custard w/green stripe	35.00- 45.00
	#2	1 lb. McKee red Dots	75.00- 85.00
	#3	1 lb. McKee Delphite blue	100.00-125.00
	#4	1 lb. McKee yellow bottom, crystal top	10.00- 12.00
ROW 6:	#1	Sanitary Cheese Preserver, round	30.00- 32.00
	#2	Square cheese preserver	25.00- 30.00
	#3	Blue cheese dish (possibly foreign)	80.00-100.00
	#4	Pink cheese dish (possibly foreign)	50.00- 60.00

CHURNS, COFFEE GRINDERS, COFFEE POTS, & DISPENSERS (REFRIGERATOR TYPE)

The churns and coffee grinders are self explanatory, but note the red Silex coffee pot in Row 1 on Page 92. It is quite unusual because it is true red glass and not flashed-on like the ones in Row 2.

The refrigerator water dispensers shown on page 93 are being sought by more collectors. The transparent blue in the top row is not common. It is closer to "Fire-King" blue than "Mayfair" blue; be on the lookout for one of them.

Page 91
ROW 1:	#1	Orvus butter churn (P&G)	$ 40.00- 50.00
	#2	Electric coffee grinder (Kitchen Aid)	25.00- 30.00
	#3	Daisey churn No. 60	35.00- 40.00
ROW 2:	#1	Keystone beater	45.00- 55.00
	#2	Daisey churn No. 20	30.00- 35.00
	#3	Monarch Finer Foods churn	30.00- 35.00
	#4	Glass egg beater	32.00- 35.00
ROW 3:	#1	"Crystal" coffee grinder w/embossed ("Crystal") glass	85.00-100.00
		Same w/o original glass	40.00- 50.00
	#2	Jewel Beater, Mixer, Whipper & Freezer	35.00- 40.00

Page 92
ROW 1:	#1	Silex, w/lid, large	85.00- 95.00
	#2	Silex, "2 cupper, drip model"	15.00- 18.00
	#3	Red Silex, marked on bottom and band at center	100.00-125.00
	#4	Silex dripolator	35.00- 40.00
ROW 2:	#1	Blue band dripolator w/sugar creamer, set	30.00- 35.00
	#2	Flashed red set: dripolator/creamer/sugar/carafe	35.00- 45.00
ROW 3:	#1	Cory coffee maker	15.00- 20.00
	#2	McKee Glasbake dripolator	40.00- 50.00
	#3,4	Glasbake ring decorated pots, ea.	20.00- 25.00

Page 93
ROW 1:	#1	L.E. Smith cobalt blue water dispenser	250.00-300.00
	#2	Same, light blue	125.00-150.00
	#3	McKee white dispenser	85.00-100.00
ROW 2:	#1	McKee Jade Green dispenser, 5¼" tall	110.00-135.00
	#2	McKee Jade Green dispenser	75.00- 85.00
	#3	McKee custard dispenser	85.00-100.00
ROW 3:	#1	McKee w/Jade Green top	125.00-150.00
	#2	Sneath Glass Co. green clambroth w/crystal top	45.00- 55.00
	#3	Water dispenser, Jade Green top	35.00- 45.00

CRUETS

Cruet collectors mix the whole range of "Elegant" glassware to "junque" in their quest for colors and designs. Note that several of these are missing stoppers and the price should be reduced because of that. All prices are for cruets with good stoppers, even though they may not be shown in the photograph.

The Jadite at the end of Row 2 should have a stopper instead of a cork, but it is an unusual find. A friend drove several hundred miles to an auction and paid a "goodly sum" for an experimental blue Heisey cruet as shown in Row 3: #2. It is not Heisey and may be Imperial although I have been told that it is U.S. Glass.

ROW 1:	#1	Fostoria yellow "Trojan"	$200.00-225.00
	#2	Fostoria blue "Fairfax"	100.00-125.00
	#3	Fostoria amber "Fairfax"	75.00- 85.00
	#4	Fostoria green "Mayfair"	60.00- 75.00
	#5	Same, yellow	60.00- 75.00
ROW 2:	#1	Fostoria "Colony"	30.00- 35.00
	#2	Fostoria yellow "Baroque"	200.00-225.00
	#3	Paden City pink #210 line	40.00- 45.00
	#4	Same, green	40.00- 45.00
	#5	Jadite "Vinegar"	65.00- 75.00
ROW 3:	#1	U.S. Glass (?) set on tray	70.00- 85.00
	#2	U.S. Glass (?) blue (not Heisey experimental blue)	65.00- 75.00
	#3	Same as #1, pink	80.00- 95.00
	#4	Pink	40.00- 45.00
ROW 4:	#1	U.S. Glass green	35.00- 40.00
	#2	Same, crystal	15.00- 18.00
	#3	Same, pink	40.00- 45.00
	#4	Imperial, pink	40.00- 45.00
	#5	New Martinsville "Janice" blue	35.00- 40.00
	#6	New Martinsville "Radiance" crystal	15.00- 20.00
ROW 5:	#1	Cambridge green	25.00- 27.00
	#2	Same, amber	25.00- 27.00
	#3	Cambridge, "Caprice" blue	45.00- 50.00
	#4	Cambridge, "Apple Blossom" pink	65.00- 75.00
	#5	Cambridge, amber in Faberware	20.00- 25.00

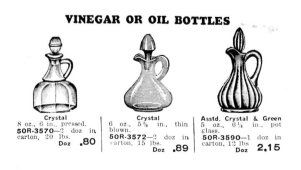

VINEGAR OR OIL BOTTLES

Crystal
8 oz., 6 in., pressed.
50R-3570—2 doz in carton, 20 lbs.
Doz .80

Crystal
6 oz., 5¾ in., thin blown.
50R-3572—2 doz in carton, 15 lbs.
Doz .89

Asstd. Crystal & Green
5 oz., 6¼ in., pot glass.
50R-3590—1 doz in carton, 12 lbs
Doz 2.15

CRUETS Continued

Notice the predominance of pink and green on the Cruet pages. If you collected blue or red, you might not add to your collection very often; and they will sock your pocketbook harder than the other colors.

I can't go any further without commenting on Row 2: #3. Everyone who has seen the pictures for this book is intrigued by this pink cruet which is probably foreign. It is most unusual in design.

ROW 1:	#1	Imperial "Canary Yellow" (vaseline)	$45.00-	50.00
	#2	Imperial green	30.00-	35.00
	#3	Imperial "Cape Cod"	22.00-	25.00
	#4	Imperial ribbed and beaded, pink	35.00-	40.00
	#5	Same, no beads	30.00-	35.00
	#6	Heisey, crystal	30.00-	35.00
ROW 2:	#1	Lancaster Glass Company, yellow	60.00-	75.00
	#2	Same, green	40.00-	50.00
	#3	Pink blown (probably foreign)	60.00-	70.00
	#4	Imperial pink	35.00-	45.00
	#5	Fostoria "Garland"	40.00-	50.00
	#6	Amber	30.00-	35.00
ROW 3:	#1	Heisey "Old Sandwich" w/stopper	65.00-	75.00
	#2	Heisey "Yeoman"	50.00-	60.00
	#3	Heisey "Twist", 4 oz., "Moongleam" green	75.00-	85.00
	#4	Same, "Flamingo" pink	65.00-	75.00
	#5	Same, 2½ oz.	60.00-	70.00
	#6	Imperial "Cape Cod"	15.00-	20.00
	#7	Duncan "Caribbean" blue	50.00-	60.00
ROW 4:	#1	Duncan "Canterbury"	15.00-	20.00
	#2	Red	75.00-	95.00
	#3	Green	40.00-	50.00
	#4	Imperial's "Verde" green from Heisey "Crystolite" mold	15.00-	20.00
	#5	Hazel Atlas green	25.00-	30.00
	#6	Same, pink	35.00-	40.00
ROW 5:	#1,2	U.S. Glass (?) dark green, ea.	30.00-	35.00
	#3	Pink	25.00-	30.00
	#4	Green	25.00-	30.00
	#5	Crystal	18.00-	20.00
	#6	Hocking green	22.00-	25.00

DISPENSERS, DRINK and JUICE

You need lots of room and lots of money to collect these counter items from old stores. Many collectors stop with one or two for their bar. The most commonly found ones are the Mission Fruit Juice, but others can be found with patience. More of these are found at advertising items shows than at any other place. People who collect advertising items found these before collectors of kitchenware did. Now, you have to beat everyone else to the next show in your area.

You will note a couple of repeated items shown here, but one of the newer pictures was a disaster and to use the old one meant duplicating a couple of dispensers. I felt it was better to do that than to miss the chance to show the other items.

Page 99
ROW 1:   #1   Samovar yellow (possibly Paden City) $200.00-250.00
          #2   Mission Orange   150.00-175.00
          #3   Mission Grapefruit   200.00-250.00

ROW 2:   #1   Paden City perculator, 3 piece, green (also amber)   100.00-150.00
          #2   Mission Real Fruit Juice (pink)   85.00-100.00
          #3   Mission Real Fruit Juice (green)   110.00-125.00

Page 100
ROW 1:   #1   Nesbitt green   65.00- 75.00
          #2   Mission Orange   150.00-175.00
          #3   Nesbitt pink   125.00-135.00

ROW 2:   #1   Lash's (also w/black lid)   150.00-175.00
          #2   Welch-Ade (Lid embossed "Welch-Ade 10¢")   100.00-125.00
          #3   Mission Grapefruit pink   85.00-100.00
          #4   Mission Grapefruit green   110.00-125.00

ROW 3:   #1   Fowler's Cherry Smash   200.00-225.00
          #2   Nesbitt's California Grapefruit   65.00- 75.00

Page 101
TOP ROW:
          #1   Bireley's Orange Juice   200.00-225.00
          #2   Amber barrel and green base   150.00-175.00
          #3   Samovar green (possibly Paden City)   175.00-200.00

BOTTOM ROW:
                Orange Crush   150.00-175.00

101

FUNNELS, GRAVY BOATS & ICE BUCKETS

Several collectors suggested I find some new categories for this book, so you can see a couple of new ones here: gravy boats and ice buckets. Both of these categories stretch from "Elegant" glass to "junque" so I tried to show examples of both this time. If more collectors get started in these areas, I will expand it even further next time. The ice buckets would be the easiest to start, but realize, before long, they can take up a lot of space! Remember I warned you.

Page 103

ROW 1:
#1 Funnel, 11", crystal	$ 20.00-	25.00
#2 Funnel, 9", crystal	15.00-	20.00
#3 Funnel, 5", crystal	10.00-	12.00
#4,5 Funnel, 4" or 4½", crystal, ea.	6.00-	9.00

ROW 2:
#1,2 Funnel, 4½", ribbed or plain green	35.00-	40.00
#3 Funnel, 4½", plain pink	45.00-	50.00
#4 Funnel, yellow canning	35.00-	50.00
#5 Funnel, Tufglas	75.00-	85.00

ROW 3:
#1 Funnel, Radnt	50.00-	60.00
#2 Cambridge green gravy and platter	45.00-	50.00

ROW 3 (Continued)
#3 Duncan "Festive" gravy and ladle	$ 30.00-	40.00

ROW 4:
#1 Imperial, red gravy and platter	125.00-	150.00
#2 Same, pink w/o platter	18.00-	20.00
#3 Same, blue w/o platter	35.00-	40.00

ROW 5:
#1 Cambridge, double gravy w/o platter	22.50-	25.00
#2 Same, pink	22.00-	25.00
#3 Same, blue	30.00-	35.00
#4 Cambridge cream sauce boat for asparagus platter	20.00-	22.50

Ice Buckets
Page 104

ROW 1:
#1 Jeannette "Hex Optic" w/reamer top, green	$35.00-	40.00
#2 Van Deman "Black Forest", pink	45.00-	50.00
#3 Fostoria "Polar Bear"	25.00-	30.00
#4 McKee, green	20.00-	25.00

ROW 2:
#1 Fostoria "Swirl", blue	25.00-	30.00
#2 Fostoria "Colony"	45.00-	50.00
#3 Cambridge etched grapes	30.00-	35.00
#4 Fostoria, yellow	30.00-	40.00

ROW 3:
#1 Fostoria, pink	25.00-	30.00
#2 Fenton, jade	35.00-	40.00
#3 Same, black	40.00-	50.00
#4 Pink w/etched flower and square bottom	25.00-	30.00

ROW 4:
#1 Cambridge, "Decagon", amethyst	$ 35.00-	40.00
#2 Same, amber	25.00-	30.00
#3 Cambridge, green	25.00-	30.00
#4 Cambridge, #731 or "Rosalie", blue	50.00-	55.00

ROW 5:
#1 Hocking "Frigidaire Ice Server"	10.00-	12.50
#2 Hocking, "Ring"	12.00-	15.00
#3 Paden City (?) pink	22.00-	25.00
#4 Crystal, Made in U.S.A. (English, other languages on side	8.00-	10.00

Page 105

ROW 1:
#1 Fry w/lid, pink	$ 60.00-	75.00
#2 Same, green	175.00-	200.00
#3 Fenton, w/lid, yellow	75.00-	85.00
#4 Fenton, w/lid, jade	75.00-	85.00

ROW 2:
#1 Cambridge "Mt. Vernon", red	75.00-	85.00
#2 Fenton, w/lid, green	55.00-	60.00
#3 Fenton "Plymouth", red	50.00-	60.00
#4 Green w/metal lid	20.00-	22.50

ROW 3:
#1 Pink "Diamond"	22.50-	25.00
#2 Green "Zig-Zag"	20.00-	22.50
#3 Green	18.00-	20.00
#4 Paden City "Party Line" w/etched flowers, pink	25.00-	30.00

ROW 4:
#1 Paden City "Party Line", pink	$ 25.00-	30.00
#2 Same, amber	22.00-	25.00
#3,4 Paden City "Cupid", green or pink	55.00-	65.00

ROW 5:
#1 Paden City "Cupid" ice tub, pink	50.00-	55.00
#2,3 Paden City "Party Line" ice tub, ea.	22.00-	25.00
#4 Green ice tub	16.00-	18.00

KNIVES

Difficulty in photographing these glass knives did not allow for a new photograph this time. The photographer has promised a new format for the next time. Hopefully, the pink will look pink and not amber as it does in this picture.

I attended an auction of Akro Agate in August of 1985 where two glass knives sold. I know from the accounting books of the Akro factory that they made glass knives. The knives sold at that auction were supposedly Akro. One of those I know was not. The other one could have been and would answer the question of who made the AER-FLO. The forest green knife I bought at the auction is exactly the shade of green of Akro's Jade in the children's sets of the same period. Since we did not reshoot the knives, the forest green one will not be shown until next time. Sorry.

			CRYSTAL	BLUE	GREEN	PINK
ROW 1:	#1,3	3 Star, 9¼″	$ 8.00-10.00	$17.50-20.00	---	$16.00-18.00
	#2,4	3 Star, 8½″	8.00- 10.00	17.50-20.00	---	16.00-18.00
	#5,9	5 Leaf Dur-X, 9¼″	8.00- 10.00	17.50-20.00	16.00-18.00	14.00-16.00
	#6,8	3 Leaf Dur-X, 8½″	8.00- 10.00	17.50-20.00	16.00-18.00	14.00-16.00
	#7	3 Leaf Dur-X, 9¼″	8.00- 10.00	---	---	14.00-16.00
	#10	Plain handle, 9¼″	---	---	22.00-25.00	---
	#11	Plain handle, 8¼″	---	---	22.00-25.00	---
	#12	Steel-ite, 8½″	20.00-22.00	---	50.00-55.00	50.00-55.00
ROW 2:	#1	J.C.W., 9″	12.00-14.00	---	---	---
	#2	Plain, 8¾″	12.00-14.00	---	---	---
	#3	No marking, 8¼″	12.00-14.00	---	---	---
	#4	Pat 12/14/20 esp, 9¼″	---	---	28.00-30.00	---
	#5	B.K. Co. Lemons, 9¼″	18.00-20.00	---	---	---
	#6	B.K. Co. Flowers, 9¼″	16.00-18.00	---	---	---
	#7	Candlewick, 8½″	55.00-65.00	---	---	---
	#8	Dagger	45.00-50.00	---	---	---
	#9	Pinwheel, 8½″	8.00-10.00	---	---	---
	#8-10	Block, 8¼″	8.00-10.00	---	20.00-22.00	20.00-22.00

			AMBER	CRYSTAL	GREEN	PINK
ROW 3:	#1-4	Stonex, ribbed handle, 8¼″*	45.00-55.00	---	25.00-30.00	45.00-55.00
	#5-8	AER-FLO, 7½″**	45.00-55.00	10.00-12.00	25.00-30.00	18.00-20.00
	#9	Westmoreland thumb-guard, 9¼″	---	45.00-50.00	---	---
	#10	Westmoreland, flowers	---	20.00-25.00	---	---
	#11	Westmoreland, miniature	---	40.00-45.00	---	---
	#12	Butter, red handle	---	18.00-20.00	---	---
	#13	Butter, green handle	---	18.00-20.00	---	---

*Opalescent White $50.00-55.00
**Forest Green $55.00-65.00 also found in box marked Quickut handy

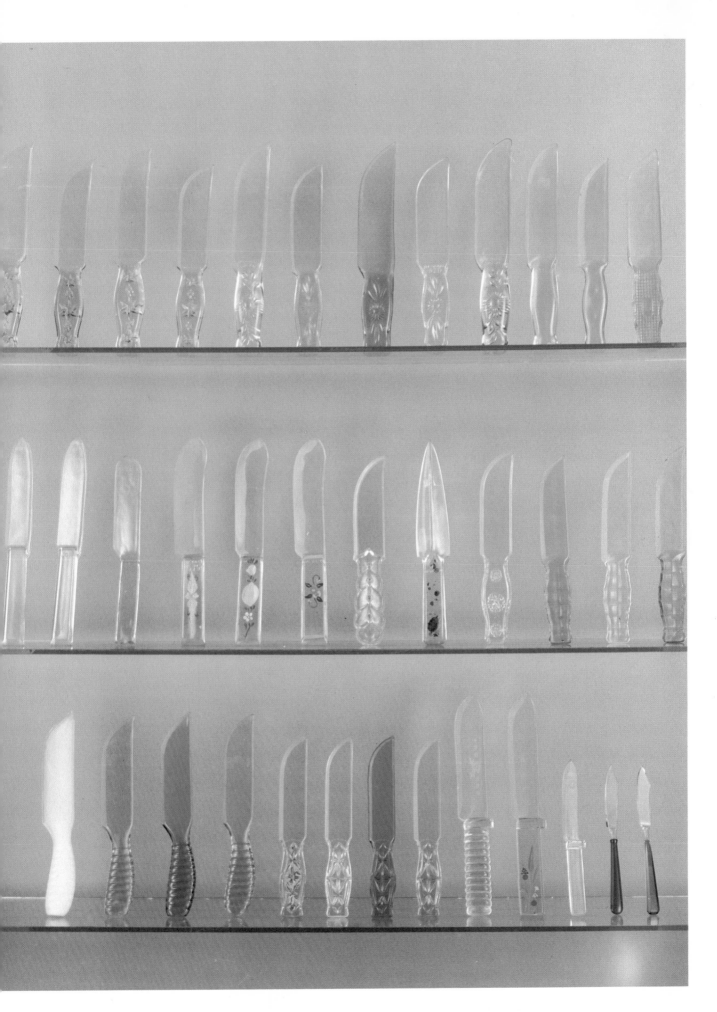

LADLES

There are sundry glass ladles to be found bearing Depression era colors because many of the dishes of the da[...] were sold with their own serving ladle. Occasionally, a ladle turns up with an extra glob of glass (pontil residue[...] where someone failed to grind it off. These are more novel than rare.

The marked Heisey Alexandrite ladle, Row 1, page 111, is the most costly one pictured; however, ladles in black[...] cobalt, red and light blue are good, as are unusual colored ladles in opaline and various opaques.

Page 109
ROW 1:
#1-3 Black	$ 22.00-	25.00
#4-7 Pink	6.00-	8.00
#8,9 Amethyst	20.00-	22.00

ROW 2:
#1-3 Light blue	12.00-	15.00
#2 Light blue "Radiance"	22.00-	25.00
#4 Iridized blue	18.00-	20.00
#5,6 Cobalt blue	30.00-	35.00
#7 Cobalt blue etched	35.00-	38.00
#8,9 Crystal	3.00-	4.00

ROW 3:
#1-7 Green	$ 6.00-	8.00
#8 Frosted green w/flowers	12.00-	14.00
#9 Clambroth green	12.00-	15.00
#10 Clambroth dark green	12.00-	15.00

ROW 4:
#1-3 Amber dark	10.00-	12.00
#4 Amber w/crystal handle	14.00-	16.00
#5-7 Yellow	12.00-	14.00
#8 Frosted yellow	8.00-	10.00
#9,10 Fired-on yellow and black	3.00-	5.00

Page 110
ROW 1:
#1 Large w/red handle	$ 30.00-	35.00
#2 Crystal punch	12.00-	15.00
#3 Large w/amber handle	22.00-	25.00

ROW 2:
#1,3 White punch	18.00-	20.00
#2 Crystal punch, Duncan "Caribbean"	25.00-	30.00

ROW 3:
#1 Clambroth w/metal plug which makes it a dry measure	$ 15.00-	18.00
#2 Black wood handle measures on side of ladle	30.00-	35.00
#3 Pickle ladle	12.00-	15.00

Page 111
ROW 1:
#1-6 Cambridge ladles-green	$ 10.00-	12.00
blue	20.00-	25.00
amber	12.00-	15.00
forest green	20.00-	22.00
pink	8.00-	10.00
#7-10 Fostoria ladles-blue	18.00-	20.00
pink	8.00-	10.00
yellow	14.00-	16.00
amber	14.00-	16.00
green (not shown)	8.00-	10.00
#11-14 Heisey ladles-green	22.00-	25.00
pink	20.00-	22.00
Alexandrite	60.00-	65.00
crystal	10.00-	12.00

ROW 2:
#1-3 2 color ladles	8.00-	10.00
#4 Crystal	3.00-	4.00
#5 Pink	6.00-	8.00
#6 Frosted crystal	5.00-	6.00

ROW 2 (Continued)
#7-9 Candlewick	$ 5.00-	6.00
#10,11 Yellow opaque or red	35.00-	40.00
#12 Opaline	28.00-	30.00
#13,14 Criss crossing design-blue	17.00-	20.00
amber	14.00-	16.00
pink or green (not shown)	8.00-	10.00
#15 Green	8.00-	10.00

ROW 3:
#1 Yellow	12.00-	14.00
#2,7 Blue	18.00-	20.00
#3 Amber	10.00-	12.00
#4 Black	22.00-	24.00
#5 Pink	6.00-	8.00
#6,9 Green	6.00-	8.00
#8 Forest green	12.00-	14.00
#10-12 White	5.00-	6.00

ROW 4:
#1-10 Crystal, ea.	3.00-	4.00

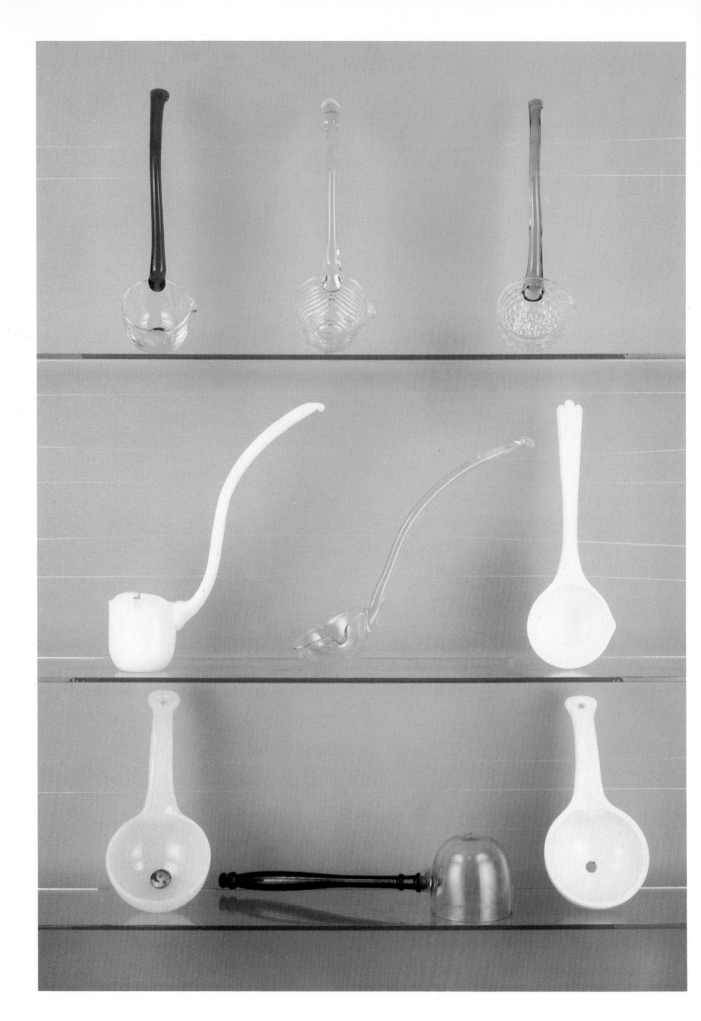

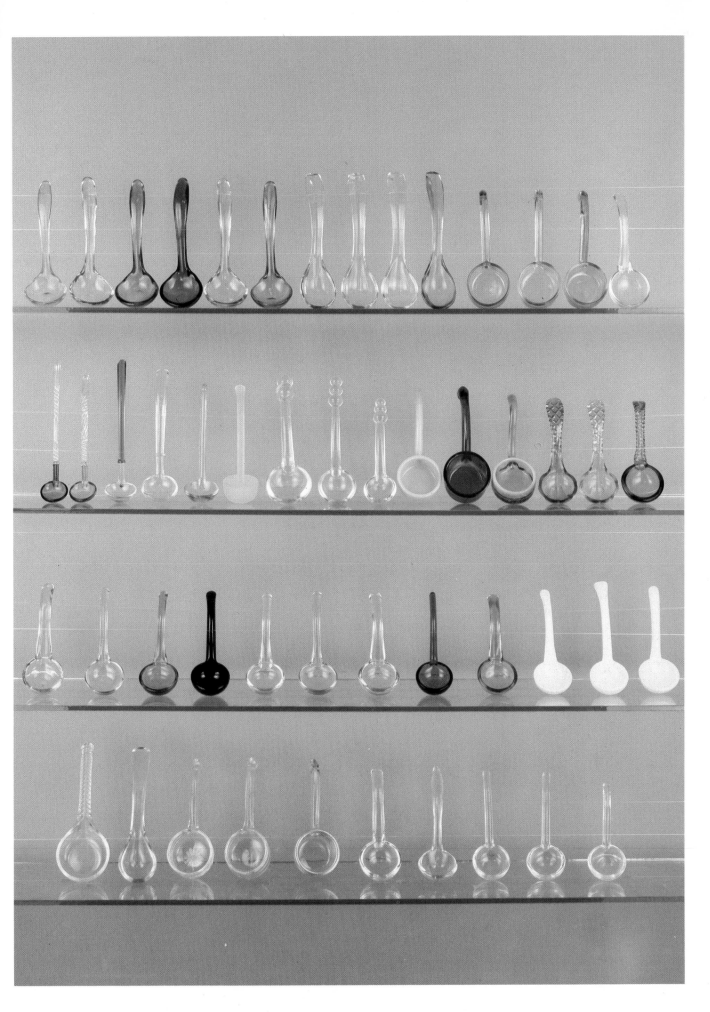

MEASURING CUPS - ADVERTISING & PATTERN GLASS

You will notice a large price range on these measuring cups. One of the major problems that I had in pricing this book, with dealers from the East and the West, was a big descrepancy in prices obtained from them. In the case of advertising cups, collectors of advertising will pay more than collectors of measuring cups. Where there is a large price range below indicates that I obtained lower prices from measuring cup collectors than I did from advertising collectors. That is just one of the things that makes pricing a book such FUN! Actually, only two people determine price - the buyer and the seller.

ROW 1: #1 "CREAM DOVE" Brand Peanut Butter Salad Dressing" Cream Dove mfg. in Binghamton, NY .... $ 15.00- 30.00
       #2 "FLUFFO", "Be sure of success, use Fluffo shortening & salad oil" 20.00- 22.00
       #3 "EASY", Combination washer/dryer with confidence built in 18.00- 20.00
       #4 "ARMOUR", Use Armour's extract of beef 18.00- 20.00
       #5 "PET MILK" Use Pet Milk, my pet cup 18.00- 20.00

ROW 2: #1 "TIPPE CANOE", Kitchen Cabinets, none better 15.00- 30.00
       #2 "Owen & Co." 15.00- 30.00
       #3 "NAPANEE" Dutch Kitchen Cabinet, world's finest kitchen cabinets, Coppes Bros. & Zook, Napanee, Ind 15.00- 30.00
       #4 "HEALTH CLUB" Baking Powder for Success in every baking 15.00- 30.00
       #5 "CLOVERDALE" quality (4 leaf clover in red) 15.00- 30.00
       #6 "ALONZOO BLISS CO.", our native herbs, Washington, D.C. 2 tbls. 10.00- 12.00

ROW 3: #1 "SILVER'S", Brooklyn, Trademark (picture Brooklyn Bridge) 15.00- 30.00
       #2 "PICKERINGS", Your credit is good, complete home furnishings, 10th & Penn, Pittsburgh 15.00- 30.00
       #3 "SELLER'S", Pat. Dec. 8, 1925 .... 15.00- 30.00
       #4 "BROWN EKBERG" Golden Rule Store 15.00- 30.00
       #5 "SAGINAW MILLING CO." 15.00- 30.00
       #6 "ROOT-TEA-NA", For health use ROOT-TEA-NA, Akron, Oh., 4 tbls. 15.00- 20.00

ROW 4: #1 "STICKNEY & POOR" Spice Co. 15.00- 30.00
       #2 Same, BOSTON 15.00- 30.00
       #3 "SILVER & CO.", 8 oz. tumbler 15.00- 25.00
       #4 "Higbee" (bee in bottom) 15.00- 25.00
       #5 Same, only dry measure 15.00- 25.00
       #6 Dry measure (cup shape) 15.00- 25.00

ROW 5: #1 Odd shade 12.00- 15.00
       #2 Log handle 15.00- 20.00
       #3 Kellogg's 25.00- 35.00
       #4 Square 15.00- 24.00
       #5 Crystal 12.00- 20.00

ROW 6: #1-3 Westmoreland w/o measure lid 35.00- 40.00
             Same w/measure lid (most have advertising in base such as "Finley Acker & Co.", highest grade at lowest cost. 60.00- 70.00
       #4,5 Measurements below spout; w/o measure lid $60.00-65.00; w/lid .. 85.00- 90.00

MEASURING CUPS

Be sure to look at the bottom row on the next page. The McKee 2-spout is the "creme de la creme" of measuring cups. They have been positioned so that you can see the shape this time. ENJOY!

ROWS 1-3 JEANNETTE SETS except ROW 2: Green $25.00-27.50; Pink $20.00-22.50

	Ultra-marine	Pink	Crystal	Delphite	Jadite
1 cup	32.00-35.00	25.00-30.00	15.00-20.00	35.00-40.00	12.00-15.00
½ cup	32.00-35.00	25.00-30.00	15.00-20.00	25.00-30.00	10.00-12.50
⅓ cup	15.00-20.00	12.50-15.00	10.00-12.50	15.00-17.50	6.00-8.00
¼	11.00-15.00	12.50-15.00	10.00-12.50	10.00-12.50	5.00-7.50
Set	90.00-105.00	75.00-90.00	50.00-65.00	85.00-100.00	33.00-43.00

ROW 4: #1 Glasbake (A.J. Novite & Sons; Charleston, 3 S.C.) $ 12.00- 15.00
    #2 Box for Jeannette set 8.00- 10.00
    #3 Fry, 1 spout 30.00- 35.00
    #4 Fry, 3 spout 45.00- 55.00
    #5 "Ideal" teas. & tbls. measure (Pat. 5/26/95) 30.00- 40.00
ROW 5: #1 McKee, crystal, 2 spout 65.00- 75.00
    #2,3 Radnt, crystal, 2 spout or Glasbake, 1 spout 40.00- 50.00
    #4,5 Glasbake, crystal, 1 spout, ea. 8.00- 10.00
ROW 6: #1-5 McKee 2 spout (turned to show from all angles): (prices below by color)

Seville Yellow	Caramel	Black	Jadite	Chalaine Blue
150.00-200.00	300.00-400.00	400.00-500.00	85.00-100.00	350.00-450.00

Page 116

ROW 1 & 2: **HOCKING GLASS Co.**
 #1 "Fire-King" 1 spout $ 10.00- 12.00
 #2 Box w/measure cup/ther-
  mometers for room/bath/food   40.00- 50.00
 #3 "Fire-King" 3 spout   12.00- 15.00
 #4,5 Green 1 spout, ea.   15.00- 18.00
ROW 2:
 #1,4 Green Clambroth, ea.   100.00- 150.00
 #2,3 Crystal, ea.   12.00- 15.00
 #5 Green   14.00- 16.00
 #6 Crystal "Fire-King"   2.00- 3.00
ROW 3:
 #1 Hocking, crystal, 3 spout   4.00- 5.00
 #2 Hazel Atlas, 3 spout, cobalt blue   300.00- 350.00
 #3 Same, yellow   175.00- 225.00
 #4 Same, unembossed pink   30.00- 35.00
 #5 Same, unembossed green   14.00- 16.00
 #6 Same, embossed "Urban's Liber-
  ty Flour"   40.00- 45.00
ROW 4:
 #1 Hazel Atlas, 3 spout, red flashed   30.00- 35.00
 #2 Same, green flashed   25.00- 30.00

ROW 4 (Continued)
 #3 Same, opalescent white $ 40.00- 45.00
 #4,5 Same, flat white, w/red trim   45.00- 55.00
 #6 Same, embossed Kellogg's, pink   18.00- 20.00
ROW 5:
 #1 Same, embossed Kellogg's, green   12.00- 15.00
 #2 Hazel Atlas, 1 spout, pink   40.00- 45.00
 #3 Same, green   25.00- 30.00
 #4 Federal, green, no hdl., 3 spout   15.00- 18.00
 #5 Same, crystal   6.00- 8.00
 #6 Same, amber   30.00- 35.00
 #7 Federal, green, 1 spout, solid
  handle   30.00- 35.00
ROW 6:
 #1 Federal, 3 spout, open handle,
  amber   30.00- 35.00
 #2 Same, pink   50.00- 55.00
 #3 Same, crystal   5.00- 6.00
 #4-6 Federal 3 spout, solid handle,
  green or crystal, ea.   22.00- 25.00

Page 117

ROW 1:
 #1 U.S. Glass 1 spout, pink $40.00- 45.00
 #2 Same, green   18.00- 20.00
 #3 U.S. Glass 3 spout, green   20.00- 22.00
 #4 U.S. Glass 1 spout, crystal   14.00- 15.00
 #5 U.S. Glass dry measure, white   125.00- 150.00
ROW 2:
 #1 U.S. Glass 2 spout, slick
  hdl./green   25.00- 30.00
 #2 Same, pink   30.00- 35.00
 #3 Dry measure, embossed E.E.
  Hamm, Hanover, Pa.   20.00- 22.00
 #4 Same, embossed Sellers   35.00- 40.00
 #5 U.S. Glass, 1 spout, slick
  hdl./grn.   45.00- 50.00
ROW 3:
 #1 Tufglas   85.00- 100.00
 #2,4 Green, 1 spout   40.00- 50.00
 #3 Amber, 1 spout   125.00- 150.00
 #5 Crystal, 1 spout   12.00- 14.00

ROW 4:
 #1 Glasbake, red flashed $ 20.00- 25.00
 #2 Glasbake, white w/red trim   45.00- 50.00
 #3 Pyrex, 1 spout   7.00- 9.00
 #4 Pyrex   3.00- 4.00
 #5 Pyrex, 2 spout   20.00- 22.00
ROW 5:
 #1 Cambridge, crystal   45.00- 50.00
 #2 Paden City, crystal   15.00- 20.00
 #3,4 Cup or dry measure embossed
  "Kanton Kitchen Kup", ea.   15.00- 20.00
 #5 Heisey cup   150.00- 175.00
ROW 6:
 #1 Crystal, oval   16.00- 20.00
 #2 Green, oval   60.00- 75.00
 #3 Blue foreign EJKRONT
  (measures tea, coffee, wine)   35.00- 40.00
 #4 Foreign (liters) etched 1895   18.00- 20.00
 #5 Foreign "Sepdelen"   75.00- 85.00

MEASURING CUPS (RARE and UNUSUAL)

The prices will indicate that not all of these are so rare or unusual, but most of them are. It was difficult to coordinate photography of these at two locations; one of the ways we tried was this split picture.

As far as 4 cup measures go, some of the unique (at this time) are shown. The McKee 4 cup Caramel and Delphite in Row 2 are the only ones known as is true with the Chalaine blue without handles in Row 3. Pricing these three cups was a problem; so I studied the prices suggested. The interesting price was from the dealer who gave the highest price for the 1-cup, 2-spout Chalaine blue for which at least five are known. He gave the lowest price quote for the 4-cup which is the only one known. That is why it is impossible for everyone to agree on what any one piece is worth and why I use a price range.

Speaking of the 4-cups sans handles, reminds me that there have not been any reports of Custard or Seville Yellow in this measuring cup. I suspect that they will turn up eventually.*

ROW 1:	#1	Cambridge dry measure, green	$150.00-175.00
	#2	Cambridge, 1 spout, 1 cup, pink	150.00-200.00
	#3	Same, green	150.00-175.00
	#4	U.S. Glass, 2 cup, pink	125.00-150.00
ROW 2:	#1	McKee, 4 cup, Caramel	200.00-250.00
	#2	Same, Delphite	225.00-275.00
	#3	Unknown, green, 2 cups = 1 pt and 20 oz. = 1 pt on side	60.00- 75.00
ROW 3:	#1	McKee, 4 cup, no handle, Jadite	125.00-150.00
	#2	Same, crystal	25.00- 30.00
	#3	Same, Chalaine blue	350.00-400.00
	#4	Tufglas, 4 cup	55.00- 65.00
ROW 4:	#1	McKee, 4 cup, Custard	20.00- 25.00
	#2	Same, Jadite	20.00- 25.00
	#3	Same, Seville yellow	45.00- 55.00
	#4	Same, Chalaine blue	100.00-125.00

* (As we go to press, Seville Yellow found!)

MEASURING CUP

1C778—8 oz., 3 in. high, heavy crystal, well finished, graduated for cups. 4 doz. in carton, 48 lbs..............Doz 48c

GLASS MEASURING CUPS

No. 3   No. 2

No. 3—Half Pint Glass Measuring Cup. Packed 2 dozen to carton.
Per dozen $1.56
No. 2—Half Pint Glass Measuring Cup. Packed 2 dozen to carton.
Per dozen $2.20

MEASURING CUPS

Emerald Green

1C2193 — 8 oz., 3 in. high, clear crystal, lipped, graduated for ounces and pints. 2 doz. in carton, 30 lbs.....Doz 78c

1C779—8 oz., 3⅛ in. high, substantial pressed emerald green glass, graduated for ounces and cups. 2 doz. in carton, 25 lbs. Doz 85c

MEASURING CUPS
CO-734 — 2 doz in carton, 18 lbs
Doz 78c
8 oz., 3⅝ in., pressed cup and ounce graduated.

1C2183—2 styles, plain and side lip, 8 oz., 3¼ in. high, clear crystal, graduated for ounces and cups. Asstd. 3 doz. in carton. Doz 79c

MEASURING PITCHERS (2 CUPS OR MORE)

There are several pitchers to note on these three pages. The green with white dots on the top row next page is not common as is true with the fired-on red in the second row. On page 123 in Row 2, the green pitcher and the Cambridge with measuring funnel top are both something you should try to find!

Page 121
ROWS 1-4 HAZEL ATLAS 2 CUPS
ROW 1:
#1-3 White w/dots	$ 30.00-	35.00
#4 Green w/white dots	40.00-	50.00
#5 Black flower decal	20.00-	22.50

ROW 2:
#1,2 White w/decorated bands	20.00-	25.00
#3 White	15.00-	18.00
#4 Opalescent white	12.00-	15.00
#5 Fired-on red	35.00-	40.00

ROW 3:
#1 Yellow	150.00-	175.00
#2 Iridized	85.00-	100.00
#3 Green	12.00-	14.00
#4 Cobalt blue	100.00-	125.00

ROW 4:
#1,2 Pink or light pink	65.00-	85.00

ROW 4 (Continued)
#3 Crystal	$ 8.00-	10.00
#4 Embossed A&J	8.00-	10.00

ROW 5:
#1 Hocking, 2 cup, ribbed, green	35.00-	40.00
#2 Same, pink	25.00-	30.00
#3 Same, crystal	12.00-	15.00
#4 Vitrock (add $10.00-15.00 for lid which fits a bowl)	18.00-	20.00

ROW 6:
#1 Hocking, 2 cup, green	12.00-	14.00
#2 Same, green Clambroth	85.00-	100.00
#3 Fire-King, 16 oz., 2 spout	15.00-	18.00
Same, crystal embossed "Diamond Crystal Shaker Salt"	20.00-	25.00
#4 Made in Italy 1971, "Grandma's Old Time Measure"	12.00-	15.00

Page 122
ROWS 1-4 ALL McKEE 2 CUPS
ROW 1:
#1,2 Ships	$ 12.00-	15.00
#3-5 Black, red bows or wild rose flower	20.00-	25.00

ROW 2:
#1,2 Red or black "Diamond Check"	20.00-	25.00
#3 Red or green dots on white	20.00-	22.50

ROW 3:
#1,2 Fired-on green or jadite	10.00-	12.50
#3 Delphite	40.00-	55.00
#4 Seville yellow	30.00-	35.00
#5 Custard	15.00-	18.00

ROW 4:
#1,2 Black or orange dots on custard	$ 22.50-	25.00
#3 Custard w/red trim	18.00-	20.00
#4 Glasbake crystal	15.00-	18.00

ROW 5:
#1 Iridized carnival	40.00-	45.00
#2 Crystal	6.00-	8.00
#3 U.S. Glass slick hdl., grn.	30.00-	35.00
#4 Same, crystal	20.00-	25.00
#5 Same, pink	35.00-	40.00

ROW 6: JEANNETTE, 2 CUP, SUNFLOWER DESIGN IN BOTTOM

Light Jadite	Dark Jadite	Delphite	Transparent Green
10.00-12.00	20.00-25.00	35.00-40.00	75.00-85.00

Page 123
ROW 1:
#1 "Ocean Mills", Montreal, Canada (Man holding box of Chinese starch), 2½ pt.	$ 60.00-	75.00
#2 "Davis Baking Powder", ½ gal.	60.00-	75.00
#3 ½ gal.	40.00-	50.00

ROW 2:
#1 1 qt.	25.00-	35.00
#2 1 qt., green	125.00-	150.00
#3 Cambridge, 1 qt, measure top	75.00-	85.00
#4 Baby formula, 20 oz., (foreign) Estans Materna	20.00-	25.00

ROW 3:
#1 Umpire Glass Co., Pittsburgh, 1 qt.	20.00-	25.00

ROW 3 (Continued)
#2 Silvers Brooklyn Trademark, 1 qt.	$ 20.00-	25.00
#3 Sanitary Bess Mixer (4 inside a large one)	175.00-	200.00
#4 Lighting Dasher Egg Beater Co., 1 pt.	18.00-	20.00
#5 Hazel Atlas 4 cup crystal	12.00-	15.00

ROW 4:
#1,2 Hazel Atlas frosted green and white w/red trim, ea.	18.00-	20.00
#3,4 Hazel Atlas A&J green or white w/black trim, ea.	20.00-	25.00

MECHANICAL ATTACHMENTS

Kitchen gadgets abound; this is only a tip of the iceberg as to what it is possible to collect from that era. You will notice that some of these have motors; but the majority were hand cranked.

Page 125

ROW 1:	#1	"Keystone" beater, Pat. Dec. 1885, North Bros.	$ 45.00- 55.00
	#2	Jewel "Beater Mixer" (mfg. by Juergens Bros., Minn., Mn.)	35.00- 40.00
	#3	Sanitary glass ice cream freezer (Consolidated Mfg. Co.)	60.00- 75.00
	#4	Mixer, 1 qt. capacity	8.00- 10.00
	#5	"Ladd" beater, green or pink (not shown)	30.00- 35.00
ROW 2:	#1	Hydraulic "Niagara" food mixer (attaches to faucet)	20.00- 25.00
	#2	Thermos (mercury lined), "Higbee Hot/Cold Sanitary Bottle"	60.00- 75.00
	#3	Criss Cross food mixer (baby face on side)	20.00- 25.00
	#4	Mixer, bands at 4-8-12 oz. marks, Kamkap, Inc., U.S.A.	8.00- 10.00
	#5	Fire-King popcorn popper	30.00- 35.00
ROW 3:	#1	"Vidrio" electric mixer w/cobalt blue base	75.00-100.00
	#2	Same, w/custard slag base	30.00- 45.00
	#3	"Chicago Electric" beater w/Jadite bottom	30.00- 35.00
	#4	"Challenge" w/Custard bottom	20.00- 25.00
	#5	"Kenmore" electric beater	20.00- 25.00

Page 126

ROW 1:	#1	Beater and jug	20.00- 22.00
	#2	Wesson Oil Mayonnaise Maker (recipe is embossed in side)	10.00- 12.00
	#3	Onion chopper	10.00- 12.00
	#4	Beater and bowl	10.00- 12.00
	#5	Ruby red beater bowl	30.00- 35.00
ROW 2:	#1	Electric beater and bowl	18.00- 20.00
	#2,3	Choppers	6.00- 8.00
	#4	Malted milk maker	12.00- 14.00
	#5	Egg & cream beater	15.00- 18.00
	#6	Electric beater	10.00- 12.00
ROW 3:	#1	Electric juicer, Sunkist	20.00- 25.00
	#2	Delphite beater bowl	25.00- 30.00
	#3	Child's glass bake egg beater	30.00- 32.00
	#4,5	Egg and cream whippers	8.00- 10.00
ROW 4:	#1	Ice cube breaker, North Bros. Mfg. Co.	25.00- 28.00
	#2	Glass sifter	50.00- 55.00
	#3	Reamer	15.00- 18.00
	#4	Electric beater	20.00- 22.00

Page 127

ROW 1:	#1	"J. Hutchanson" Trademark S&S Long Island (Mayonnaise)	100.00-125.00
	#2	Cobalt beater	75.00-100.00
	#3	Ultra-marine beater	35.00- 40.00
	#4	Pink beater	25.00- 30.00
ROW 2:	#1	"Bromo-Seltzer" dispenser	115.00-135.00
	#2	"Ladd" mixer churn #2	65.00- 75.00
	#3	Mixer (similar to Keystone)	45.00- 55.00
	#4	"Silver & Co." food mixer	20.00- 25.00
	#5	"Bordens" Pat. Mar. 30, 1915	18.00- 22.00

MUGS

There are not many mug collectors per se, but mugs do come in a great variety of colors and shapes, which makes for interesting display concepts. The split pictures were taken at two locations in order to incorporate as many different mugs as possible.

The first mug in Row 1 has the "Fire-King" design on the outside. This is normal for the blue, but very few jadite have the design. It is the design which makes this mug so expensive, since it is very common without the design.

The McKee "Bottoms-Down" in Row 4 are very popular, with the Jadite found more often than the Seville yellow. However, I would not pass either by if I found them priced reasonably. I recently bought a pair for $38.00 at an antique show set up in a local mall.

ROW 1:	#1	Fire-King, Jad-ite, (design on outside) (no design $2.00-3.00)	$ 20.00- 22.50
	#2	Fire-King, Sapphire blue	16.00- 18.00
	#3	Hocking, pretzel, green	20.00- 25.00
	#4	Same, crystal w/trim (w/o trim $3.00-4.00)	4.00- 5.00
	#5	Green (called Adam's Rib by collectors)	12.00- 15.00
	#6	Same, amber	12.00- 15.00
ROW 2:	#1	Cambridge, cobalt blue root beer	35.00- 50.00
	#2	Yellow root beer	25.00- 35.00
	#3	Imperial "Chesterfield", amber	15.00- 18.00
	#4	Green Clambroth	25.00- 30.00
	#5	Barrel shaped, "pinched" handle	30.00- 35.00
ROW 3:	#1	Green root beer	20.00- 25.00
	#2	Same, pink	20.00- 25.00
	#3	Amber	30.00- 35.00
	#4	Black, "Genolite"	25.00- 30.00
	#5	Green soda fountain type	22.00- 25.00
	#6	Peacock blue	22.00- 25.00
ROW 4:	#1	McKee "Bottoms-Down" beer mug, Seville yellow	115.00-130.00
	#2	Same, Jadite	85.00-100.00
	#3	Cambridge "Mt. Vernon", emerald green	25.00- 30.00
	#4	Cambridge 'Tally-Ho", red	22.00- 25.00
	#5	New Martinsville, red	20.00- 25.00
	#6	Imperial "Chesterfield", green	15.00- 18.00
ROW 5:	#1	New Martinsville "Moondrops", cobalt blue	25.00- 30.00
	#2	Hocking "Colonial", pink	200.00-250.00
	#3	Jeannette, footed, green	22.50- 25.00
	#4	Same, pink	22.50- 25.00
	#5	Pink as in Row 1: #5 & 6	12.00- 15.00

8-PC. BEER SETS
GREEN GLASS . . . OPTIC PATTERN

80 oz. jug, six 12 oz. handled mugs, 10 in. covered pretzel or cookie jar, pressed green glass.
50R-2075—1 set in carton, 12 lbs......**Set .95**

128

NAPKIN HOLDERS

I am glad the photographer's picture of this shows up better than mine! I take a 35mm picture to have to work with as we photograph the set ups. That is, unless I get so busy arranging, gathering for the next shot or packing the last one. Photographing glass is quite a procedure (as several collectors who have become involved will attest) and I hope you appreciate our efforts to let you see this glass.

In any case, the best napkin holder is shown below. It is U.S. Glass Company's "Paramount", worth $175.00-200.00. It also comes in green and black having approximately the same value. The black are the hardest to find, but you will note a severe lack of pink in the picture. There do not seem to be many pink napkin holders available.

ROW 1:	#1	Frosted crystal	$ 30.00- 35.00
	#2	NAR-O-FOLD, Property of trade Nar-O-Fold mark Napkin Company, Chicago, Reg. U.S.A., black	80.00-100.00
	#3	Same, white	20.00- 25.00
	#4	Emerald green	60.00- 75.00
ROW 2:	#1	Paden City "Party Line", crystal	30.00- 35.00
	#2	Same, black	80.00-100.00
	#3	Same, pink	85.00-100.00
	#4	Same, white	50.00- 65.00
ROW 3:	#1	Same, green	65.00- 75.00
	#2	SERV-ALL, white	50.00- 65.00
	#3	Same, green Clambroth	75.00-100.00
		Same, emerald green (shown in 2nd Edition)	90.00-100.00
	#4	L.E. Smith crystal	30.00- 40.00
ROW 4:	#1	SLEN-DR-FOLD, white	35.00- 40.00
	#2	Ft. Howard HANDI-NAP, white	25.00- 30.00
	#3	FAN FOLD, crystal	30.00- 40.00
	#4	Same, white	40.00- 50.00
ROW 5:	#1	Same, emerald green	80.00-100.00
	#2	Same, green	75.00- 95.00
	#3	Property of Diana Mfg., Green Bay	70.00- 90.00

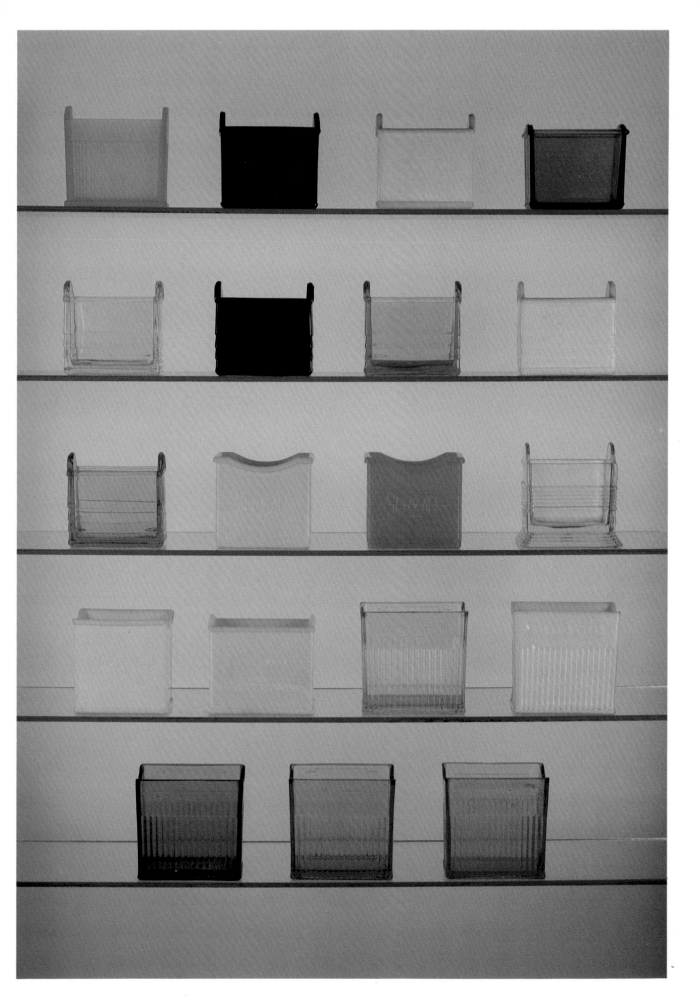

131

OIL & VINEGAR or FRENCH DRESSING BOTTLES

Most of these bottles fit the category of "Elegant" glassware. They are, for the most part, handmade, such as the Fostoria, Cambridge and Heisey, which means few are cheaply priced. You need a deep pocket or a strong checking account to collect many oil and vinegar bottles. One of the blessings is that they are not bulky and do not require as much room to display as some other collectibles.

Bottles with etchings are better than plain ones and ones with known major etchings are even better. Of course, the competition for finding these type bottles is more fierce.

ROW 1:	#1	Paden City, green	$ 37.50- 42.50
	#2	Same, pink	35.00- 40.00
	#3	Cambridge, etched pattern, green	75.00- 85.00
	#4	Same, no etching	35.00- 40.00
	#5	Cambridge, amber w/crystal stopper	30.00- 35.00
	#6	Same, w/amber stopper	35.00- 45.00
	#7	McKee set (late 1940's)	15.00- 20.00
ROW 2:	#1	Cambridge "Rosalie" (#731), pink	75.00- 85.00
	#2	Same, green	80.00- 90.00
	#3,5,7	Cambridge crystal, ea.	15.00- 18.00
	#4	Cambridge w/sterling stopper	30.00- 35.00
	#6	Hawkes, green	50.00- 60.00
ROW 3:	#1	Heisey, "Flamingo" pink	50.00- 65.00
	#2	Same, crystal ("Mfg. under license granted by T.G. Hawkes & Co.	30.00- 35.00
		Fill w/vinegar to line marked Vinegar, w/oil to line marked Oil, salt & pepper, etc., to taste, shake & you have perfect dressing")	
	#3	Heisey "Twist", pink	55.00- 70.00
	#4,9	Fostoria amber, ea.	30.00- 35.00
	#5	Fostoria w/sterling top	20.00- 22.00
	#6,7	Fostoria, yellow or green	75.00- 85.00
	#8	Fostoria yellow w/crystal top	45.00- 50.00
ROW 4:	#1	Paden City "Party Line", pink	45.00- 50.00
	#2	Unknown "pyramid" style (2 style stoppers)	35.00- 40.00
	#3	Cambridge set, 3 pc. pink	35.00- 45.00
	#4	Crackle set (possibly Cambridge)	35.00- 40.00
	#5	Yellow	22.50- 25.00
	#6	Cambridge pink	15.00- 20.00
	#7	Amber	22.00- 25.00

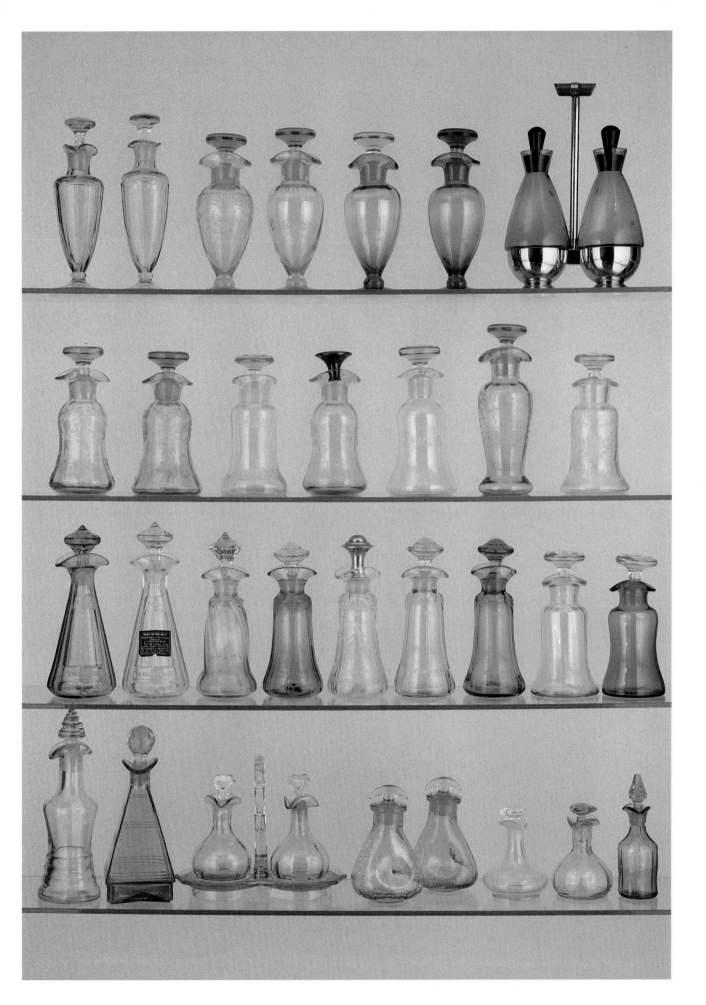

RANGE SETS

These little rounded Hocking Vitrock range sets have graced many a kitchen over the years! As you can see, they were made in various colorful designs and they came bearing labels of flour, cereal, sugar, drippings, etc. They are easily incorporated into today's decor.

Today, the blue and red lidded sets seem to be the most popular with collectors.

ROW 1:	#1	"Blue Circle w/Flowers" (5 piece set)	$ 22.00- 25.00
		Same, grease or drippings jar	10.00- 12.00
		Same, shakers, ea. (not shown)	4.00- 5.00
	#2-6	"Blue Circle" (5 piece set)	30.00- 32.00
		Same, grease jar	14.00- 18.00
		Same, shakers, ea.	4.00- 5.00
ROW 2:	#1,2	"Red Tulip" (5 piece set)	22.00- 25.00
		Same, grease jar	10.00- 12.00
		Same, shakers, ea.	4.00- 5.00
	#3-6	"Black Circle" (5 piece set)	25.00- 28.00
		Same, grease jar (not shown)	12.00- 14.00
		Same, shakers, ea.	4.00- 5.00
	#7	"Black Circle w/Flowers" (5 piece set)	22.00- 25.00
		Same, grease jar	10.00- 12.00
		Same, shakers, ea. (not shown)	4.00- 5.00
ROW 3:	#1,2	"Green Flower Pots" (5 piece set)	26.00- 30.00
		Same, grease jar	12.00- 15.00
		Same, shakers, ea.	4.00- 5.00
	#3-7	"Red Flower Pots" (5 piece set)	16.00- 20.00
		Same, grease jar	10.00- 12.00
		Same, shakers, ea.	4.00- 5.00
ROW 4:	#1,7	"Red Circle w/flowers" (5 piece set)	24.00- 28.00
		Same, grease jar, screw-on lid (rare)	22.00- 25.00
		Same, grease jar, regular glass lid	10.00- 12.00
		Same, shakers, ea. (not shown)	4.00- 5.00
	#2-6	"Red Circle" (5 piece set)	26.00- 30.00
		Same, grease jar (not shown)	12.00- 15.00
		Same, shakers, ea.	4.00- 5.00
ROW 5:	#1-3	Hazel Atlas, set of 3, black or green letters	25.00- 30.00
		Shakers, ea.	5.00- 6.00
		Grease jar	15.00- 18.00
	#4	Same as above (red letters)	22.00- 25.00
	#5-7	Set of 3	25.00- 30.00
		Shakers, ea.	5.00- 6.00
		Grease jar	15.00- 18.00
	#8	Green grease jar	20.00- 22.00
		Jar w/o lid	6.00- 7.50

NO. HW324R—30 OZ.
RANGE JAR & COVER

Packed 2 doz. ctn. wt. 28 lbs.

List
Less Carton Lots **$2.64 Doz.**
Full Carton Lots **2.40 Doz.**

NO. HW323R—9 OZ. SALT &
PEPPER SHAKERS—Dec. **Red**

Pkd. 1 doz. prs. ctn. wt. 11 lbs.

List
Less Carton Lots **$3.60 Doz. Pr.**
Full Carton Lots **3.28 Doz. Pr.**

REAMERS - BABY

The smaller reamers are very popular and fit the space limitations of many collectors. You can get quite a few of these on a shelf if you can afford them.

In Row 3, I have included the newly made "Barnes" reamer made from the old Westmoreland mold. Only the two colors shown have been made at present, but others will follow. Both the top and bottom are marked with a "B" in a circle. This should not cause any problems for anyone if you are careful and know from whom you are purchasing your glass.

WESTMORELAND GLASS COMPANY (ROWS 1-3)

ROW 1:	#1	Pink, 2 piece	$115.00-140.00
	#2	Same, crystal	75.00- 85.00
	#3	Blue (bottom only $90.00-100.00)	175.00-200.00
	#4	Amber, 2 piece	150.00-200.00
	#5	Sun-colored-amethyst (bottom only $40.00-45.00)	80.00- 90.00
	#6	Green, 2 piece	150.00-200.00

ROWS 2 & 3 Bottom is worth ⅔ of price except where noted below.

ROW 2:	#1	Frosted pink	100.00-120.00
	#2	Green (top and bottom about equal in value)	175.00-200.00
	#3	Crystal w/decorations	35.00- 40.00
	#4	Pink (bottom value $20.00-25.00)	85.00-100.00
	#5	Frosted blue bottom only	40.00- 45.00
	#6	Sun-colored-amethyst (SCA)	60.00- 70.00

ROW 3:	#1	Frosted crystal (decorated add $10.00)	50.00- 60.00
	#2	Pink decorated	100.00-115.00
	#3	Blue (bottom value $25.00-30.00)	125.00-150.00
	#4,5	NEW! RUBINA AND COBALT BLUE MARKED WITH B IN CIRCLE INSIDE CONE OF TOP AND ON BOTTOM OF BASE (Vaseline color made as we go to press)	12.00- 15.00

ROW 4:	#1	L.E. Smith (top rare), pink	150.00-200.00
	#2	Same, green	150.00-200.00
	#3	Same, crystal (in metal add $5.00)	20.00- 30.00
	#4	Jenkins, green	90.00-100.00
	#5	Same, crystal	25.00- 35.00
	#6	Same, frosted crystal	35.00- 45.00

ROW 5:	#1	Unknown, blue (top $200.00)	300.00-350.00
	#2	Unknown, pink (top $100.00)	150.00-175.00
	#3	Unknown, crystal (top $10.00)	20.00- 25.00
	#4	Unknown, frosted crystal "Baby's Orange"	60.00- 75.00
	#5	Unknown, crystal	25.00- 35.00
	#6	Unknown, frosted crystal decorated "Baby"	75.00- 85.00

ROW 6:	#1	Unknown, crystal	30.00- 40.00
	#2	Unknown, crystal, called "Button & Bows"	40.00- 50.00
	#3	Unknown, crystal probably foreign (emb. sword & hammer)	25.00- 35.00
	#4	Unknown, crystal, "thumbprint" design	40.00- 50.00
	#5	Unknown, crystal, notched top	40.00- 50.00
	#6	Unknown, crystal	30.00- 40.00

ROW 7:	#1	Unknown, decorated crystal, "Orange Juice"	50.00- 60.00
	#2	Unknown, frosted decorated crystal	85.00-100.00
	#3	Unknown, pink (possibly foreign)	100.00-125.00
	#4	Fenton, SCA (sun-colored-amethyst) (bottom $50.00)	60.00- 75.00
	#5	Fenton, elephant decorated base	60.00- 75.00

REAMERS - CAMBRIDGE, EASLEY, FEDERAL, FOREIGN, FENTON & FRY

The cobalt blue Cambridge reamer on the next page is still the only one to turn up in that color. The foreign reamers on page 140 have a whole collecting field to themselves. There are many unique shapes and colors to attract a collector. The Fenton pitcher and reamer tops on page 141 are still among my favorites. The blue set has found its way from the home of the grand-daughter of a Fenton factory worker in Louisville, Ky., to southern California via Houston, Texas.

Page 139

ROW 1:
#1 Cambridge, cobalt blue, "Pat. Jan 6, 1909" (crys. $20.00-25.00) $1500.00- 2000.00
#2 Cambridge, green 200.00- 250.00
#3 Same, crystal 10.00- 12.50
#4 Crystal 12.00- 14.00

ROW 2:
#1 "Easley pat Pend" (called "chisel cone") 50.00- 75.00
#2 "Easley pat July 10, 1888; Sep. 10, 1889" 20.00- 30.00
#3 "Easley pat. July 10, 1888" 15.00- 20.00
#4 "Easleys pat. July 10, 1888; Sep. 10, 1889; 8.00- 12.00
#5 "Easleys July 10, 1888; Sep. 10, 1889; 8.00- 12.00

ROW 3:
#1 "Easley's New Model May 11, 1909 No. 4" (SCA) 10.00- 20.00

Foreign Reamers

Page 140

ROW 1:
#1 Pinkish amber .... $ 40.00- 45.00
#2,5 Cobalt blue or amber 85.00- 95.00
#3 Smoke 75.00- 85.00
#4 Yellowish custard 80.00- 90.00

ROW 2:
#1,5 Pink or light pinkish amber 40.00- 50.00
#2,3 Embossed "Foreign", 2 piece, green or pink 35.00 40.00
#4 Yellow 100.00- 125.00

ROW 3:
#1,3,5 Root Beer, blue and light yellow, ea. 85.00- 95.00
#2 Embossed "Tcheco-Scovaquie" on handle, crystal 40.00- 50.00
#4 Embossed sword and hammer on handle 15.00- 20.00

ROW 4:
#1,5 Crystal, last has "K" inside shield mark, ea. 15.00- 20.00

FENTON GLASS COMPANY

Page 141

ROW 1:
#1 Fenton pitcher and reamer set, blue $1000.00- 1200.00
#2 Same, black 600.00- 750.00
#3 Same, red 600.00- 750.00
#4 Same, jade (top only $75.00-100.00) 400.00- 500.00

ROW 2:
#1,2 Fenton, 2 piece, rabbit decals (plain $40.00-50.00) 80.00- 100.00
#3 Same, pink (bottom only $60.00-75.00) 150.00- 200.00
#4 Fenton, "Ming" (bottom only $90.00-100.00) see pg. 46 .... 250.00- 300.00
#5 Blue opalescent 100.00- 135.00

FRY GLASS COMPANY

ROW 3:
#1 Straight side, opalescent (emb. "Blue Goose" $150.00-175.00) 12.00- 15.00

ROW 3 (Continued)
#2 Same, crystal .... $ 5.00- 10.00
#3 "Easley's improv'd, Mar. 6, 1900" 10.00- 12.00

FEDERAL GLASS COMPANY

ROW 4:
#1 Ribbed, loop handle, amber 17.50- 20.00
#2 Same, pink 20.00- 22.50
#3 Tab handle, seed dam, no ribs, green 6.00- 10.00

ROW 5:
#1 Panelled, loop handle, amber 15.00- 18.00
#2 Same, green 20.00- 25.00
#3 Tab handled, ribbed, seed dam, amber 12.00- 14.00
#4 Same, pink 85.00- 100.00

ROW 6:
#1 Tab handle, plain side, green 8.00- 12.00
#2 Same, crystal 3.00- 5.00
#3 Same, amber 200.00- 300.00

ROW 4 (Continued)
#2 Light yellow top only .... $ 60.00- 70.00
#3,4 Pink or "Coke" bottle green 40.00- 55.00

ROW 5:
#1,2,4,5 Light green, amber, amethyst or pinkish amber, ea. 40.00- 50.00
#3 Crystal 25.00- 30.00

ROW 6:
#1 Light turquoise 40.00- 45.00
#2 Green, marked "Argentina" 125.00- 135.00
#3,5 Cornflower blue or light green 90.00- 100.00
#4 Crystal, embossed fruit 50.00- 60.00

ROW 7:
#1,2 Crystal Czechoslovakia or pink 40.00- 50.00
#3,4 Light turquoise or diamond shaped crystal (Rb No 517385) 35.00- 40.00
#5 Pink 80.00- 90.00
#6 Amber 85.00- 100.00

ROW 3 (Continued)
#2 Same, vaseline yellow (emb. "Bak-rite Cinn., Oh. $150.00-200.00) .... $ 35.00- 45.00
#3 Same, emerald green 28.00- 35.00
#4 Same, light green 12.00- 15.00

ROW 4:
#1 Same, pink 35.00- 50.00
#2 Same, amber 200.00- 250.00
Same, cornflower blue (shown pg. 25) 300.00- 350.00
#3 Ruffled top, opalescent 30.00- 35.00

ROW 5:
#1 Same, vaseline yellow 150.00- 200.00
#2 Same, emerald green 200.00- 250.00
#3 Same, pink 125.00- 175.00

REAMERS - HAZEL ATLAS GLASS COMPANY

The cobalt blue reamers are the ones you wish to find made by this company. There are others that are valuable, but the blue are the prized ones.

The 2-cup pitchers of Hocking and Hazel Atlas are often confused. It is easy to distinguish these if you remember that the Hazel Atlas pitchers are embossed "Measuring and Mixing cup" in the bottom and Hocking's are plain.

Except for the green pitcher in Row 2, the pitchers are harder to find than the reamer tops and represent ⅔ of the total value.

ROW 1:	#1	"Crisscross" orange, cobalt blue	$150.00-165.00
	#2	Same, pink	150.00-200.00
	#3	Same, crystal	3.00- 5.00
		Same, green shown on pg. 202	8.00- 10.00
	#4	"Crisscross", lemon, pink	225.00-275.00
		Same, green (not shown)	8.00- 10.00
		Same, crystal (not shown)	3.00- 5.00
ROW 2:	#1	2 cup pitcher and reamer set, yellow	200.00-250.00
	#2	Same, pink	125.00-150.00
	#3	Same, cobalt blue	200.00-250.00
	#4	Same, green (shown w/o reamer top)	18.00- 22.00
ROW 3:	#1	White w/trim, 4 cup pitcher and reamer	28.00- 32.50
	#2	2 cup pitcher and reamer set, white w/trim	25.00- 30.00
	#3	4 cup pitcher only	15.00- 18.00
	#4	4 cup marked A & J with top	30.00- 35.00
ROW 4:	#1	Tab handle, lemon, green	5.00- 8.00
	#2	Same, pink	40.00- 45.00
	#3	Same, white w/red trim	20.00- 22.50
	#4	Tab handle, lemon, green	7.00- 10.00
ROW 5:	#1	Tab handle, orange, cobalt	175.00-200.00
	#2	Same, green	7.00- 10.00
	#3	Same, pink	25.00- 30.00
	#4	Same, white Clambroth	75.00- 90.00

REAMERS - HOCKING and INDIANA GLASS COMPANIES

Blue is the exciting color in Hocking, also. However, it is "Mayfair" blue or "cornflower" blue, as non-Depression collectors call it, instead of cobalt blue.

The "Mayfair" blue measuring cup and reamer set in Row 4 fills in the gap of 2-cup Hocking measures on page 121 where this cup was not shown.

The flashed-on black always stops collectors in their tracks until they determine that it is not true black.

HOCKING GLASS COMPANY

ROW 1:	#1	Reamer pitcher, green	$15.00- 18.00
	#2	"Circle" pitcher w/reamer top, green	40.00- 50.00
	#3	Ribbed 2-cup pitcher w/top, green	45.00- 50.00
	#4	Same, pink, pitcher only	25.00- 30.00
ROW 2:	#1	Loop handle orange, "Mayfair" blue	500.00-600.00
	#2	Same, green	15.00- 20.00
	#3	Same, white, embossed "Vitrock"	20.00- 22.50
		Same, unembossed	8.00- 10.00
	#4	Tab handle, green Clambroth	75.00-100.00
ROW 3:	#1	Loop handle orange, ribbed, green	12.00- 15.00
	#2	Same, "Coke" bottle green	15.00- 18.00
	#3	Same, flashed black	12.00- 15.00
	#4	Tab handle, green	10.00- 12.00
ROW 4:	#1	2-cup pitcher w/reamer top, green	18.00- 20.00
	#2	Same, "Mayfair" blue	600.00-750.00
	#3	Same, "Vitrock" white	20.00- 22.50
	#4	Indiana green	10.00- 12.50
ROW 5:	#1	Indiana amber	150.00-200.00
	#2	Same, pink	85.00-100.00
	#3	Same, green	25.00- 35.00

G640—Jug and G8—Reamer

G638—Measuring Jug and G8—Reamer

W13—ORANGE REAMER
Pkd. 2 doz. ctn.—wt. 39 lbs.

W688—1 PINT PITCHER
Pkd. 2 doz. ctn.—wt. 26 lbs.

W8—FRUIT JUICE REAMER
Pkd. 2 doz ctn.—wt. 20 lbs.

REAMERS - JEANNETTE GLASS COMPANY

As you can see by Row 2, the light Jadite colored top for the light pitcher is not to be found. Evidently, it is more difficult to find than the darker shade although the dark Jadite has a higher dollar value.

The transparent green, 2-cup pitcher with sunflower design in the bottom in Row 2 is the most desirable Jeannette reamer shown.

ROW 1:	#1	"Hex Optic" bucket reamer, green	$40.00- 45.00
	#2	Same, pink	45.00- 50.00
ROW 2:	#1	2-cup pitcher w/sunflower in bottom, green	125.00-140.00
	#2	Same, dark Jadite	35.00- 40.00
	#3	Same, light Jadite	25.00- 30.00
	#4	Large, loop handle, crystal	5.00- 8.00
ROW 3:	#1	Same, yellowish Jadite	75.00- 90.00
	#2	Same, light Jadite	15.00- 18.00
	#3	Same, dark Jadite	30.00- 35.00
	#4	Same, green	12.00- 15.00
ROW 4:	#1	"Jennyware", pink	50.00- 65.00
	#2	Same, ultra-marine	55.00- 70.00
		Same, crystal (not shown)	60.00- 75.00
	#3	Small loop handle, dark Jadite	25.00- 28.00
	#4	Same, Delphite blue	45.00- 60.00
ROW 5:	#1	Large, 5⅞", tab handle, pink	25.00- 28.00
	#2	Same, green	18.00- 20.00
	#3	Small, 5" tab handle, pink	30.00- 40.00
	#4	Same, green	18.00- 22.00

Ⓓ **Juice Extractors**
7 in., large size for oranges and grapefruit.
5OR-3305—3 doz. in carton, 55 lbs........Doz **1.75**
Less quantity, Doz **1.90**

REAMERS, SUNKIST, McKEE & MISCELLANEOUS

McKee Glass Company made most of the Sunkist reamers, though not all. The McKee symbol is an "McK" with a circle around it and said insignia adds interest to a reamer. Collectors of reamers concern themselves with color, type (lemon, orange, grapefruit), handles, spouts, seed dams or no, footed or flat bottomed, embossing, size and shape of the reaming section, etc. As usual, scarcity and demand determines price for reamers, many of which are not cheap!

Sunkist
Page 149

ROW 1:
#1 Black	$325.00-	375.00
#2 Chocolate	300.00-	425.00
#3 Crown Tuscan	150.00-	200.00
#4 Butterscotch	125.00-	175.00

ROW 2:
#1 Caramel	175.00-	225.00
#2 Caramel fry (meaning opalescence)	350.00-	500.00
#3 White "BLOCKED" (refers to lettering of Sunkist)	40.00-	50.00
#4 Chalaine blue, dark	125.00-	155.00

ROW 3:
#1 Chalaine blue, light	125.00-	175.00
#2 Turquoise blue	150.00-	200.00
#3 Dark jadite opaque	150.00-	175.00
#4 Jadite, dark, embossed	16.00-	22.00

ROW 4:
#1 Jadite, dark, unembossed	$ 40.00-	50.00
#2 Jadite, light	15.00-	20.00
#3 Forest green	350.00-	400.00
#4 Apple green	30.00-	35.00

ROW 5:
#1 Seville yellow	40.00-	45.00
#2 French ivory	30.00-	35.00
#3 Custard, dark	25.00-	28.00
#4 Custard, light	22.00-	25.00

ROW 6:
#1 Opalescent white ("Fry")	35.00-	85.00
#2 White w/caramel swirl	100.00-	200.00
#3 Pink	35.00-	50.00
#4 White (embossed Thatcher Mfg. Co.)	10.00-	15.00

McKEE GLASS COMPANY
Page 150

ROW 1:
#1 White w/red trim, small, 5¼", embossed "McK"	$ 30.00-	35.00
#2 Same, Skokie Green	12.00-	15.00
#3 Same, white	25.00-	30.00

ROW 2:
#1 Custard, small, 5¼", unembossed, pointed cone	25.00-	30.00
#2 Same, Skokie Green	28.00-	32.00

ROW 3:
#1 Custard, large, 6", embossed "McK"	30.00-	35.00
#2 Delphite, small, embossed "McK"	175.00-	225.00
#3 Same, custard	30.00-	35.00

ROW 4:
#1 White, large, embossed "McK"	$ 30.00-	35.00
#2 Custard, large, unembossed	35.00-	40.00
#3 Same, Skokie Green	25.00-	28.00

ROW 5:
#1 Grapefruit, jadite	95.00-	110.00
#2 Same, Chalaine blue	250.00-	300.00
#3 Same, Seville yellow	175.00-	200.00

ROW 6:
#1 Same, transparent green	250.00-	350.00
#2 Same, black	300.00-	400.00
#3 Same, pink	350.00-	450.00

Miscellaneous
Page 151

ROW 1:
#1 Fenton pitcher and reamer set, jade	$ 400.00-	500.00
#2 Saunders, black	650.00-	700.00
#3 Same, Jadite	600.00-	650.00

ROW 2:
#1 Cambridge, pink	100.00-	150.00
#2 Same, green	150.00-	200.00
#3 Same, amber	450.00-	550.00

ROW 3:
#1,3 Indiana, green or pink	40.00-	50.00
#2 Same, amber	100.00-	150.00

ROW 4:
#1 U.S. Glass, slick handled, amber	$250.00-	300.00
#2 U.S. Glass, 2 pc., "Aunt Polly" blue (base only)	150.00-	200.00
#3 Unknown, white	125.00-	150.00
#4 Cambridge, SCA	30.00-	40.00

ROW 5:
#1 McKee, large, 6", embossed "McK", delphite	250.00-	300.00
#2 McKee, grapefruit, Custard	200.00	250.00
#3 Same, Caramel	400.00-	500.00

REAMERS MECHANICAL

Mechanical reamers do not seem to draw as many collectors to them as do some of the more exotic reamers such as the Saunders. The "Mayfair" blue shown below was probably made by Hocking. I liked it for the color. It was found in its original box in Florida if memory serves me correct. In any case I received a wide range of prices on it from collectors of reamers. I guess it falls into the category that you either "like" it or "hate" it.

The other mechanicals on the next page are not commonly found, but are, also, not much in demand. I have often wondered how many gallons of citrus juice has been scattered over kitchens of years gone by using that first reamer. It looks as if it were made to scatter juice rather than extract it.

The Sunkist bowl on the next page appears to have lost some of its desirability over the last few years. Maybe reamer collectors decided that is was not really a part of their collecting world. Lack of demand has slowed its previously escalating price.

Top Picture			
	#1	Metal insert	$ 35.00- 45.00
	#2	Glass insert	150.00-200.00
	#3	Mount Joy	100.00-125.00
Bottom Picture			
		Sunkist bowl	175.00-200.00
		Blue Reamer below	150.00-300.00

REAMERS - PADEN CITY

The cocktail shaker bottoms shown in Row 1 & 2 are difficult to sell without the metal reamer top. If you happen to find a top for sale because the bottom was broken, do not let it slip by you. You will always be able to find a topless shaker sometime in the future.

There is a collector who would love to find a black top to go on that black pitcher shown in the bottom row. If you happen to find it let me know and I'll pass the word along.

ROW 1:	#1	Cocktail shaker/reamer, green etched, (see inverted top next)	$75.00- 85.00
	#2	"Party Line", frosted turquoise	85.00-100.00
	#3	Footed juice for above shaker	4.00- 5.00
	#4	"Party Line", turquoise, cut floral design	100.00-125.00
	#5	Same, pink	75.00- 85.00
	#6	Same, orangish pink, gold band	90.00-100.00
ROW 2:	#1	Cocktail shaker/reamer, green floral cut, called "Speakeasy"	30.00- 35.00
	#2	Same, turquoise w/o floral cut	35.00- 40.00
	#3	"Party Line" tumbler	4.00- 5.00
	#4	"Party Line" set, 4-cup pitcher and top, turquoise	150.00-200.00
	#5	Same, amber	200.00-250.00
ROW 3:	#1	Pitcher and reamer top	150.00-200.00
	#2	"Party Line" black pitcher	125.00-150.00
		Green top only ($50.00-60.00) set in green	90.00-100.00
	#3	Same, pink floral cut	100.00-110.00
	#4	Same, w/o cutting	85.00- 95.00

REAMERS - U.S. GLASS COMPANY, TUFGLAS & ORANGE JUICE EXTRACTORS

There are several traits that distinguish U.S. Glass reamers. The simple slick handle is exhibited on page 158 but note that all 2-piece pitcher types on page 157 have a ledge inside the pitcher for the insert to rest upon.

The pitcher sets shown in the top row on the next page and in yellow on page 83 are difficult to find. Note how the reamer sits upside down with a lid to cover it. Sloppy handling over the years diminished the quantities of those available!

Page 157
ROW 1:
#1 Pitcher, reamer and top $175.00-225.00
#2 Same, pink   200.00-235.00
    Same, yellow (shown on pg. 83)   400.00-500.00
#3 Tumbler to match pink set   10.00- 12.50
#4 4-cup pitcher, snowflake design in bottom, 2 piece, green   40.00- 50.00
ROW 2:
#1,2 2-cup pitcher set, open handle, green, two shades, ea.   75.00- 90.00
#3 Same, pink (bottom only $50.00-60.00)   125.00-150.00

ROW 3:
#1 5⅛" pitcher set, turquoise $ 90.00-100.00
#2 Same, white   100.00-125.00
#3 Same, green   30.00- 35.00
#4 Same, amber   250.00-300.00
ROW 4:
#1 Same, pink   30.00- 40.00
#2 Crystal, w/fruit (no fruit $12.00-15.00)   20.00- 25.00
#3,4 Same pink w/fruit or cut design   35.00- 45.00

Page 158
ROW 1:
#1 "Handy Andy", green, (metal only $8.00-10.00) $ 50.00- 55.00
#2 "Servmor", green   50.00- 60.00
#3 Slick handle, green   25.00- 30.00
#4 "Handy Andy" w/o metal (note different reamer cone)   40.00- 45.00
ROW 2:
#1 Slick handle, vertical ribbed or bars, green   40.00- 50.00
#2 Same, used for "Handy Andy"   8.00- 10.00
#3 "Vidrio Products Corp.", Chicago, Ill. green   150.00-165.00
#4 Slick handle, horizontal ribs, turquoise   75.00- 85.00

ROW 3:
#1,2 Same, green or pink $ 25.00- 30.00
#3 Same, amber   150.00-200.00
#4 "Log" handle, lemon   18.00- 22.00
ROW 4:
#1 Slick handle, frosted, pink   28.00- 33.00
#2 Same, green   23.00- 28.00
#3 Slick handle, seed dams in pour spout, green   250.00-300.00
ROW 5:
#1 Slick handle, white   40.00- 50.00
#2 Same, pink   85.00-100.00
#3 Same, green   50.00- 65.00

Page 159
ROW 1:
#1,2 Tufglas, dark or light $ 55.00- 65.00
#3 Same, blue cast   100.00-125.00
ROW 2:
#1 Pink, West Coast type   135.00-160.00
#2 Same, green   110.00-135.00
#3 White   30.00- 35.00
ROW 3:
#1 "Orange Juice Extractor", light green   50.00- 60.00
#2 Same, green   40.00- 50.00
#3 Same, pink   75.00- 85.00
#4 Same, black amethyst   200.00-225.00

ROW 4:
#1 Crystal, "Orange Juice Extractor" $ 12.00- 15.00
#2 U.S. Glass, crystal   8.00- 10.00
#3 Tab handle, green   40.00- 50.00
#4 Same, SCA   15.00- 20.00
ROW 5:
#1 Tab handle, green   10.00- 12.50
#2 Same, white   30.00- 35.00
#3 U.S. Glass, white   30.00- 35.00
#4 U.S. Glass, "Orange Juice Extractor", white   20.00- 25.00

REAMERS - West Coast

I do not see many of these in my part of the country and it was exciting to see so many at one time at my photography session in California. I can only point out some basic information on these since some of them I had never seen.

Row 1 shows a crystal insert for a Remora and a opalescent white RE-GO base. The wooden peg allows the insert to be turned by hand to extract the juice so that the glass parts do not rub together. The RE-GO comes from a reamer that originally said "puRE GOld". (The small letters in pure gold were there for emphasis by me) These were not marketed and the letters "p,u and l,d" were removed to leave RE-GO. By the way, you can see the missing letters upon looking closely at the reamer. A very complete removal of the letters was not accomplished.

The green "EASY SQUEEZE" which is shown as an insert on the right of the top row has a base which works similar to the RE-GO.

The "Fleur-de-Lis" in Row 4 and 5 are only a sampling of these special finds.

ROW 1:	#1	Crystal insert for REMORA (pat. pend.)	$150.00-200.00
		Complete	300.00-400.00
	#2	Opalescent white (Fry) RE-GO base	225.00-250.00
		Complete	450.00-500.00
	#3	RE-GO, green (base $250.00-300.00; top $150.00-200.00)	400.00-500.00
	#4	"EASY SQUEEZE" top only	200.00-225.00
		Same, base ($250.00-275.00); complete	450.00-500.00
ROW 2:	#1	"LINDSAY", green	350.00-400.00
	#2	"LINDSEY", pink	300.00-350.00
	#3	"VALENCIA", pinkish amber unembossed	150.00-200.00
		Same, embossed "VALENCIA"	150.00-200.00
ROW 3:	#1	Same, white embossed	70.00- 85.00
		Same, unembossed	35.00- 40.00
	#2	Same, green embossed	125.00-150.00
		Same, unembossed	65.00- 75.00
	#3	Same, crystal embossed	80.00-100.00
		Same, unembossed	40.00- 50.00
	#4	Same, amber embossed	200.00-300.00
		Same, unembossed	125.00-150.00
ROW 4:	#1	"Fleur-de-Lis" unembossed custard (rim around top)	125.00-150.00
	#2	Same, white	40.00- 60.00
	#3,4	Same yellowish-red slags	275.00-350.00

ROW 5: All of these are "Fleur-de-Lis" (price determined by the color as shown)

	#1	Slag	300.00-400.00
	#2	Predominately red	400.00-600.00
	#3	Opalescent amberina	500.00-600.00
	#4	Slag	275.00-350.00

REAMERS - WESTMORELAND and OTHERS

The pitchers in the top row have an embossed lemon on one side and an embossed orange on the other side. It is hard to believe, but the crystal one is the hardest one to find! This is rarely true; and even when it is, the price is usually under that of the colors.

In Row 2 & 3, the amber and white reamers are both difficult to find; and Row 4 shows four different Clambroth variations.

The bottom row shows a green "Radnt" and the pink "Tricia" with crystal top. You can see a complete pink one on page 71. The black "Tricia" is also worthy of mention as we close out the reamer section this time.

Reamer collectors have a national club and the address is National Reamers Collectors Association, % Terry McDuffee, 11830 S. Mt. Vernon Ave., Grand Terrace, Ca. 92324.

ROW 1:	#1	Westmoreland, embossed lemon/orange, 2 piece, pink	$135.00-155.00
	#2	Same, green	145.00-165.00
	#3	Same, crystal	150.00-175.00
ROW 2:	#1	*Westmoreland, flattened loop handle, amber	175.00-225.00
	#2	Same, pink	70.00- 85.00
	#3	Same, crystal, decorated	60.00- 75.00
ROW 3:	#1	Same, white	200.00-250.00
	#2	Same, light green	95.00-120.00
	#3	Same, dark green	100.00-125.00
ROW 4:	#1	Clambroth, shaped like "boat"	185.00-235.00
	#2	U.S. Glass, "Orange Juice Extractor", Clambroth	70.00- 95.00
	#3	Clambroth, tab handle	70.00- 90.00
	#4	"MacBeth-Evans Glass Co., Charleroi, Pa."	300.00-350.00
ROW 5:	#1	"RADNT", green or pink (not shown)	300.00-350.00
	#2	"Tricia" pink bottom ($150.00-200.00) complete	400.00-450.00
		Same, crystal top ($50.00-75.00) complete	200.00-225.00
	#3	Same, black (top $125.0-150.00) (bottom $275.00-350.00)	400.00-500.00
		Same, green (not shown)	300.00-400.00
	#4	"RADNT", crystal	70.00- 85.00

* Beware! This has just been reproduced in cobalt blue and vaseline with other colors sure to follow!

REFRIGERATOR CONTAINERS

Page 165

ROW 1:	#1	Pyrex, 4¼″ x 6¾″, blue & white ($4.00-5.00); blue	$ 12.00-	15.00
	#2	Same, 3½″ x 4¾″, blue & white ($2.00-3.00); blue	8.00-	10.00
	#3	Same, red ($4.00-5.00); crystal "Crosley Shelvador"	4.00-	5.00
	#4	Green, 4″ x 4″, leaf design	12.00-	15.00
ROW 2:	#1	Federal, pink 4″ x 4″ ($6.00-8.00); 4″ x 8″(15.00-18.00); 8″ x 8″	25.00-	30.00
	#2	Same, 4½″ round, pink ($12.00-15.00); white 5½″ round	6.00-	8.00
	#3	Same, 4½″ round, amber ($6.00-8.00); 8″ x 8″($12.00-14.00); 4″ x 4″)	6.00-	8.00

HAZEL ATLAS GLASS COMPANY

ROW 3:	#1	5¾″ round, flat knob, green ($15.00-20.00); cobalt blue	40.00-	45.00
	#2	5¾″ round, pointed knob, decorated	12.00-	15.00
	#3	Same as #1, white	10.00-	12.00
	#4	5″ round, white w/green leaf	6.00-	8.00
ROW 4:	#1	"Crisscross", blue, 4″ x 4″ ($18.00-20.00); 4″ x 8″ ($50.00-55.00); 8″ x 8″	60.00-	70.00
	#2	Same, 3½″ x 5¾″, crystal ($10.00-12.00); green	30.00-	35.00
	#3	Same, 5¼″ round, pink	40.00-	50.00
	#4	4½″ x 5″ pink ($18.00-20.00); yellow ($20.00-25.00); green ($12.00-14.00); blue	35.00-	40.00

Page 166

ROW 1:	#1	Fry, 4½″ x 8″	25.00-	30.00
	#2	Glassbake, 4¼″ square, light blue	3.00-	4.00
	#3	Same, 4½″ x 5″, crystal	8.00-	10.00
	#4	Green Clambroth, 3⅝″ square	6.00-	8.00
ROW 2:	#1	McKee, 4″ x 5″ red "Dots" ($10.00-12.00); Delphite ($22.50-25.00); blue "Dots", 5″ x 8″	18.00-	20.00
	#2	5″ x 8″ Chalaine blue ($40.00-50.00); 4″ x 5″ Custard or Seville	10.00-	12.00
	#3	5″ x 8″ Seville yellow ($18.00-22.00); 4″ x 5″ Jadite ($12.00-14.00); Chalaine	30.00-	35.00
ROW 3:	#1	Seville yellow, 7¼″ square	25.00-	30.00
	#2	Crystal, 3½″ x 5½″	12.00-	15.00
	#3	Jadite, 4¼″ beater bowl	6.00-	7.00
	#4	Jadite, 10 oz. canister	10.00-	12.00

HOCKING GLASS COMPANY

ROW 4:	#1	4¼″ x 4¾″, 2 styles, green, ea.	15.00-	17.50
	#2	Same, green Clambroth	20.00-	22.50
	#3	6″ square, green	18.00-	20.00
	#4	"Fire-King", 4″ x 4⅛″	4.00-	5.00
ROW 5:	#1	8″ x 8″, Vitrock ($22.00-25.00); 4″ x 4″, Vitrock ($8.00-10.00); green, ea.	10.00-	12.00
	#2	"Fire-King" Jad-ite, 4½″ x 5¼″ ($6.00-8.00); 5″ x 9″	10.00-	12.00
	#3	Same, blue, 4½″ x 5″	7.00-	9.00
	#4	Oval, 8″ green ($20.00-22.00); 7″ fired-on blue ($15.00-18.00); 6″ green Clambroth	15.00-	18.00
PAGE 167				
ROW 1:	#1	"Jennyware" 16 oz. round	18.00-	20.00
	#2	Glassbake 5½″ square w/lid	18.00-	20.00
	#3,4	McKee Hall's, 4″ x 5″ or 4″ x 6″, ea.	10.00-	14.00

JEANNETTE GLASS COMPANY

ROW 2:	#1	Floral, 5″ x 5″, Jadite ($16.00-18.00); 5″ x 10″	26.00-	28.00
	#2	4″ x 4″ Jadite ($8.00-10.00); Delphite	12.00-	15.00
	#3	4″ x 8″ Jadite (12.00-15.00); Delphite	20.00-	25.00
ROW 3:	#1	Floral, 4″ x 4″ green	45.00-	55.00
	#2,3	Round dish, 32 oz., Jadite ($15.00-18.00); Delphite	27.00-	30.00
	#4	Round crock, 40 oz., Jadite	30.00-	35.00
ROW 4:	#1	"Kompakt", green, 4″ x 4″ ($15.00-17.00); 4″ x 8″ (not shown)	22.00-	25.00
		Same, SCA, 4″ x 8″	12.00-	14.00
	#2	Jennyware, 4½″ square pink ($12.00-14.00); ultra-marine	14.00-	16.00
	#3	Same, 4½″ x 9″, pink ($20.00-22.00); ultra-marine	22.00-	24.00
ROW 5:	#1	"Hex Optic", 6″ round base ($12.00-15.00); lid ($8.00-10.00); 3 piece	30.00-	35.00
	#2	Same, 4½″ x 5″, green, base ($6.00-8.00); lid ($8.00-10.00); 3 piece	20.00-	26.00
	#3	Radnt jar, 5″ lid, and 5½″ tall	18.00-	22.00
	#4	Ultra-marine 4″ x 4″ (12.00-15.00); 4″ x 8″	20.00-	25.00

ROLLING PINS

There are no crystal $8.00-12.00 rolling pins shown this time as there is a multitude of these available and they do not show up very well with all the colored ones. I hope that does not upset anyone, but that is the way it is. The only rolling pin that has suffered a price setback is the white one marked "Imperial Mfg. Co., Cambridge, Ohio". There has been an abundance of these found in recent months. The Custard McKee has held its price for the quantity that has been found.

On page 170 transparent pink and green are finally shown. Both of these colors come in each style pictured. The green has a wooden pin running through the rolling pin with handles attached to the pin. The pink has screw-on handles.

The number of blown cobalt blue rolling pins is unbelievable when compared to the few found with wooden handles.

McKEE GLASS COMPANY except for last row.
Page 169
ROW 1: Note circular band opposite shaker top end.

	#1	Jadite	$175.00-200.00
	#2	Custard	125.00-150.00

ROW 2 & 3 Note smooth end opposite shaker top end on these rows.

	#1	Seville yellow	175.00-200.00
	#2	Delphite blue	225.00-275.00
ROW 3:	#1	Chalaine blue	250.00-300.00
	#2	Jadite	175.00-200.00
ROW 4:	#1	Crystal w/screw-on cobalt handles	150.00-175.00

Wooden Handles
Page 170

ROW 1:		Peacock blue (handles attached to metal rod inside pin)	125.00-150.00
ROW 2:	#1	Green transparent (handles attached to wood dowel pin)	225.00-275.00
	#2	Pink (screw-on wooden handles)	200.00-250.00
ROW 3:	#1	White (comes w/wood or metal screw-on handles), ea. marked "Imperial Mfg. Co., Cambridge, Ohio"*	30.00- 40.00
	#2	Cobalt blue (handles attached to metal rod inside pin)	225.00-275.00
ROW 4:		Clambroth white (screw-on wood handles)	125.00-135.00

Blown Rolling Pins
Page 171

ROW 1:	#1	Amethyst	75.00- 95.00
	#2	Cobalt blue	125.00-150.00
ROW 2:	#1	Amber, light	100.00-125.00
	#2	Forest green	125.00-150.00
ROW 3:	#1	Peacock blue, dark	95.00-110.00
	#2	Crystal, "Kardov Flour, Famous Self Rising"	35.00- 45.00
ROW 4:	#1	Chalaine blue	225.00-250.00
	#2	Blue, light	125.00-150.00

*Recently found in Custard $100.00-125.00

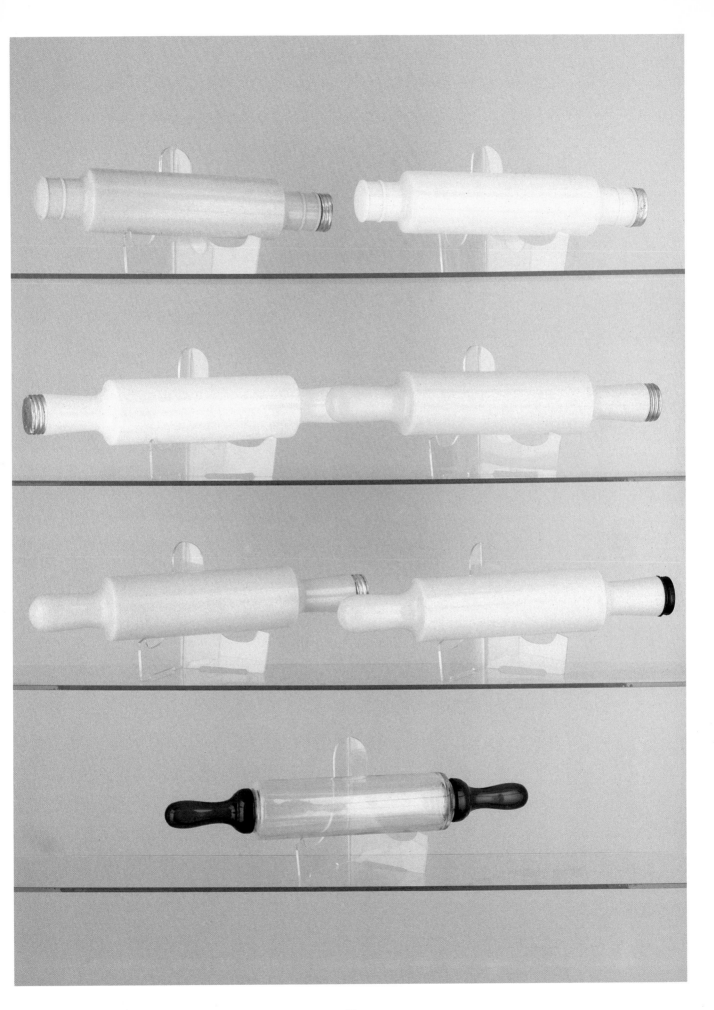

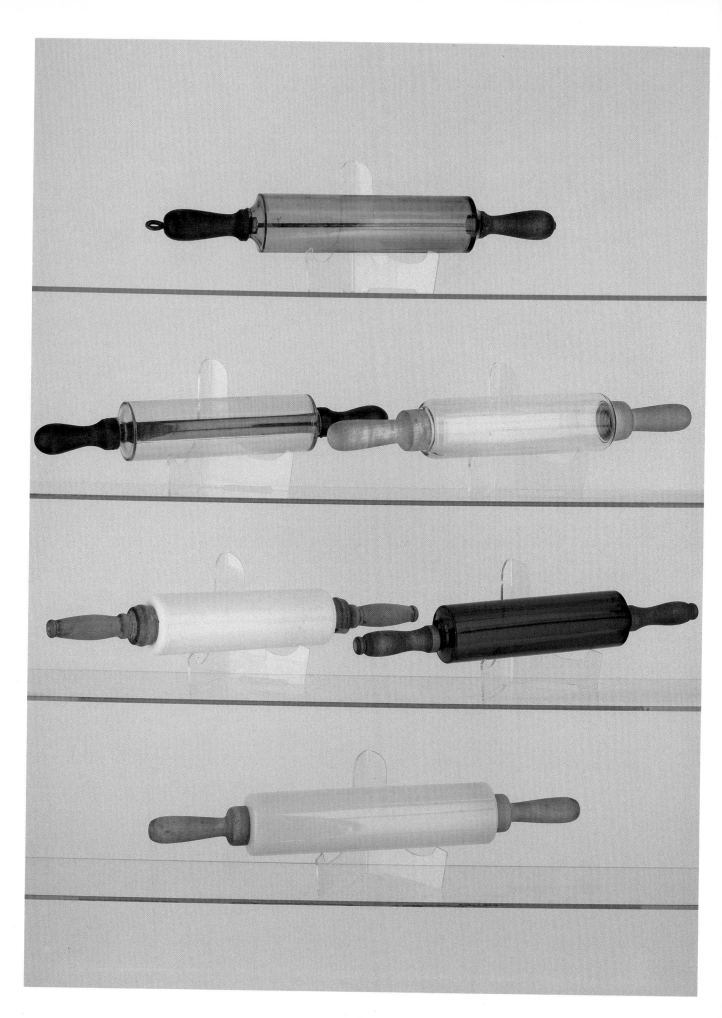

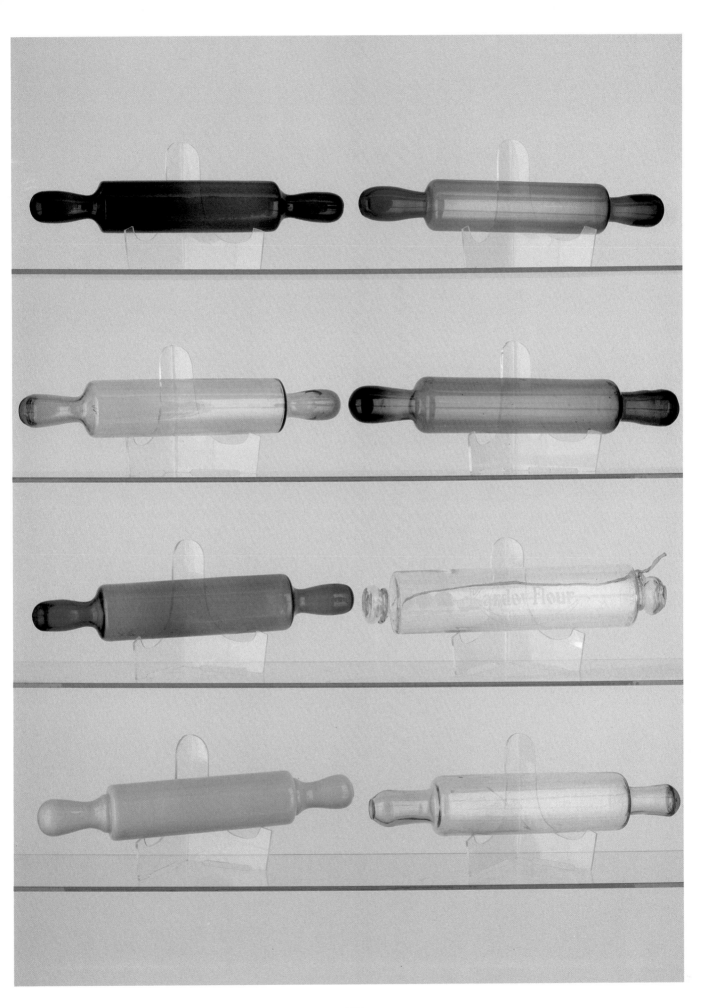

SALAD SETS

Glass salad serving sets probably reached their peak of popularity during the 1940's. Metals were needed for the war effort; so glass knives and serving pieces not only were the "elegant" way to serve guests, but in a way, it was a patriotic gesture also. The glass fork and spoon sets were very popular bridal gifts. I remember Mother used to use hers (with a kind of "Waterford" design) for serving "company" or for special Sunday dinners.

Collectors value the colored sets.

ROW 1:	#1	Crystal set, only fork shown	$ 8.00- 10.00
	#2,3	Blue handle set	35.00- 45.00
	#4,5	Green handle set	30.00- 35.00
	#6	Amber set, only spoon shown	30.00- 35.00
	#7,8	Blue handle set	35.00- 45.00
	#9,10	Amethyst handle fork and blue handle spoon set	35.00- 45.00
	#11,12	Crystal set	10.00- 12.00
ROW 2:	#1-4	Blue set	35.00- 40.00
		Amber set (not shown)	35.00- 40.00
		Green set, only fork shown	35.00- 40.00
		Crystal set, only spoon shown	7.00- 8.00
	#5,6	Crystal set	8.00- 9.00
	#7	Crystal set, only fork shown	8.00- 10.00
	#8	Crystal ladle only	20.00- 22.50
	#9	Crystal set, only spoon shown	12.00- 14.00
ROW 3:	#1	Green handle set, only fork shown	25.00- 30.00
	#2,3	Amber handle set	20.00- 22.50
		Cobalt handle set (not shown)	30.00- 32.50
	#4	Pink handle set, only fork shown	20.00- 25.00
	#5	Red handle stirring spoon	10.00- 12.00
	#6	Amber handle stirring spoon	8.00- 10.00
	#7	Red handle stirring spoon	8.00- 10.00
	#8	Pink handle fork	18.00- 20.00
	#9	Red handle knife	15.00- 20.00
	#10	Crystal Heisey spoon	12.00- 14.00
	#11	Crystal spoon	3.00- 4.00
	#12	Red handle spoon	3.00- 4.00
		Spoon holder below	150.00-165.00

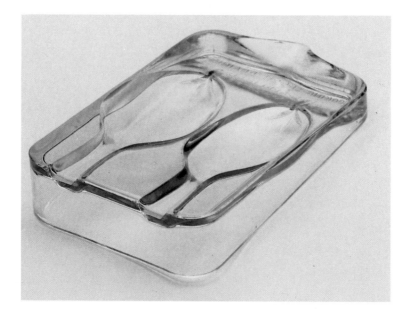

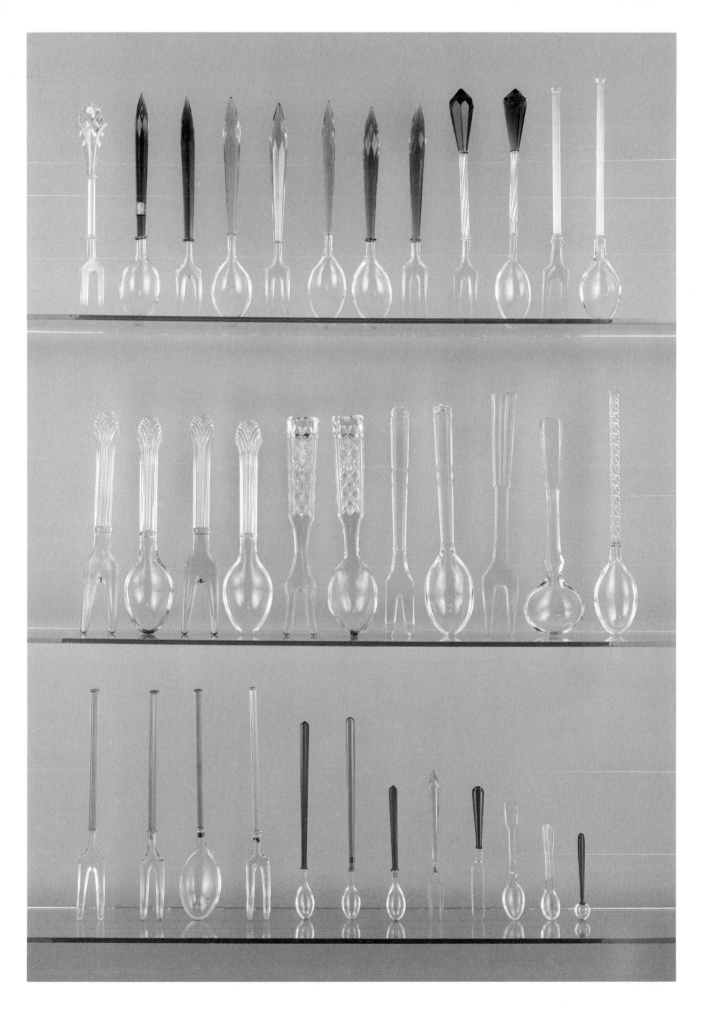

SALT BOXES

Salt boxes belong to another age, a time when you bought a coarse, heavy salt in twenty-five, fifty and hundred pound bags and used it liberally to "cure" the meat when you killed hogs, game or beef. It was a time when it was automatic to reach for a pot holder before taking hold of the iron skillet handle with one hand and getting a "pinch" of salt from the salt box with the other and "seasoning" whatever was being cooked and then dusting the salt encrusted fingers down a calico pinafore apron; a harder, yet calmer time past, still cherished in memory.

ROW 1:	#1	Hoosier cupboard type salt box, amber	$ 85.00-110.00
	#2	Same, crystal	12.00- 15.00
	#3	Same, green	100.00-125.00
	#4	Round, crystal w/o lid	8.00- 10.00
		w/wood lid	15.00- 18.00
ROW 2:	#1	Jadite w/lid, Jeannette	100.00-125.00
	#2	Crystal w/wood lid	45.00- 55.00
	#3	Crystal w/glass lid, Flintext	75.00- 85.00
	#4	White, w/wood lid, U.S. Glass	70.00- 80.00
ROW 3:	#1-3	McKee salt bowls, Jadite	75.00- 85.00
		Same, Custard	50.00- 60.00
		Same, Seville yellow	80.00- 90.00
		Same, Chalaine blue, (shown p.16)	125.00-150.00
	#4	Round crystal w/wood lid	50.00- 55.00
ROW 4:	#1-3	Jeannette round salt, top embossed SALT, green	100.00-125.00
		Same, crystal	50.00- 60.00
		Same, pink	75.00- 85.00
	#4	Crystal, rectangular, w/wood lid	55.00- 60.00
BELOW:	#1	Green "Zipper"	100.00-125.00
	#2	Green Sneath	100.00-125.00
	#3	Peacock Blue	100.00-125.00

SHAKERS

There are many collectors of shakers and I hope you will enjoy the expansion of this area. Shakers in highly collected colors and unusual markings such as "Roastmeat Seasonings" are extremely desirable. Embossed shakers are somewhat harder to find and will command premium prices also. If you find an embossed shaker in a highly collected color such as Chalaine blue, then you have an even better prize.

Shakers with popular designs such as scottie dogs or "Dutch" items are extremely collectible as are large sets of any kind. Of course, the more colorful a set is, the better it is.

ROW 1:	#1-3	Shakers, ea.	$ 2.00- 2.50
	#4	Griffith's 12 piece set in wood rack	15.00- 18.00
	#5-8	Red Tulip's, ea.	2.00- 3.00
ROW 2:	#1,2	Red Dutch shakers, ea.	4.00- 5.00
	#3,4	Dutch shakers, ea.	3.00- 4.00
	#5	Decal fruit 4 piece set on rack	10.00- 12.00
	#6,7	Windmill shaker, ea.	1.50- 2.50
	#8-10	Black lettered shakers, ea.	1.00- 1.50
ROW 3:	#1	Roastmeat Seasonings (unusual label)	5.00- 6.00
	#2,3	Refrigerator pr.	15.00- 20.00
	#4	"BALL" 12 piece spice set on rack	30.00- 35.00
	#5,6	Shaker pr. w/lady	3.00- 4.00
	#7	Shaker	3.00- 4.00
ROW 4:	#1-11	Spice set (11 of 12 pieces shown)	18.00- 20.00
	#12	Cattail	4.00- 5.00
ROW 5:	#1	Lady in blue dress	10.00- 12.00
	#2-6	Shaker, ea.	2.50- 3.50
	#7-10	Rooster shakers, ea.	3.00- 4.00

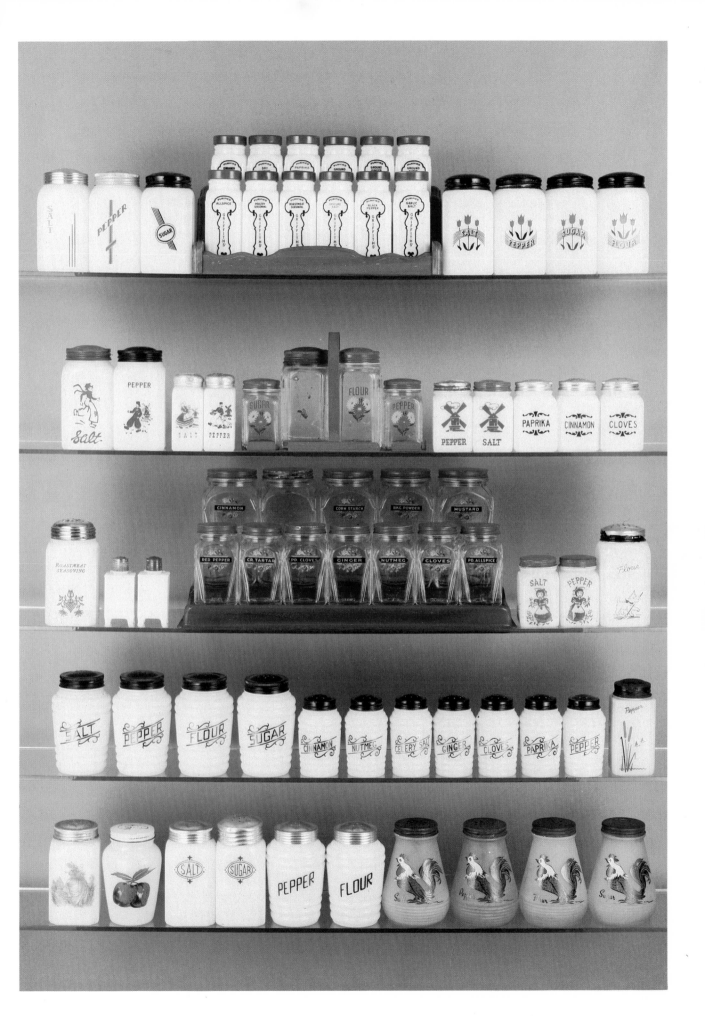

SHAKERS HOCKING, HAZEL ATLAS, OWENS ILLINOIS, TIPP CITY, ETC.

HOCKING GLASS COMPANY (ROWS 1-3)

Page 179

ROW 1:

#1-4	Opaque yellow, ea.	$9.00-	11.00
#5-7	Fired-on yellow, ea.	4.00-	6.00
#8-10	Fired-on blue, ea.	8.00-	10.00

ROW 2:

#1	Fired-on green	4.00-	6.00
#2,3	Panelled fired-on blue, ea.	8.00-	10.00
#4-6	Green Clambroth, panelled, ea.	12.00-	15.00
#7,8	Transparent green, ea.	8.00-	10.00
#9,10	Vitrock, ea.	5.00-	7.00

ROW 3:

#1	Crystal w/raised dots	4.00-	5.00
#2	Clambroth	8.00-	10.00
#3	Green, plain	9.00-	11.00
#4	Tulip (lid is valued at $1.00-2.00)	3.00-	4.00
#5,7,8	White, ea.	5.00-	6.00
#6	Green Jad-ite	4.00-	5.00
#9	Green, round	15.00-	17.50

ROW 4:

#1,2	Hazel Atlas embossed pink salt or pepper	25.00-	35.00
#3	Same, crystal	20.00-	25.00
#4,5	Same, green salt or pepper	22.00-	25.00

ROW 4 (Continued)

#6,7	Same, flour or sugar	$ 30.00-	35.00
#8	Dutch salt	10.00-	12.50
#9,10	White w/green, ea.	6.00-	8.00

ROW 5:

#1-4	White w/black	5.00-	6.00
#5,6	Black fired-on, ea.	6.00-	8.00
#7	Owens-Illinois ovoid shape (good lettering)	8.00-	10.00
#8,9	Same, square shapes	6.00-	8.00
#10,11	Sneath, amber, ea.	22.00-	25.00

ROW 6:

#1	Crystal, embossed celery	$4.00-	5.00
#2,3	Crystal, embossed salt and sugar, ea.	5.00-	6.00
#4	Green, embossed flour	35.00-	40.00
#5	Green	30.00-	40.00
#6	Clambroth	12.00-	15.00
#7	Clambroth	10.00-	12.50
#8	Black, round	15.00-	18.00
#9	Black	8.00-	10.00
#10	Black, ribbed	18.00-	20.00

Page 180

ROW 1:

#1	Tipp City 12 piece set	$ 18.00-	20.00
#2	Tipp Rangette set in box	3.00-	5.00
#3	Tipp City 12 piece set	18.00-	20.00

ROW 2:

#1	Tulips on rack	5.00-	6.00
#2-6	Basket 5 piece range set	15.00-	20.00
#7-10	Basket 4 piece set on rack	10.00-	15.00

ROW 3:

#1	Flower, 8 piece set on rack (1 missing here)	15.00-	18.00
#2	Flower, 2 piece on rack	5.00-	6.00

ROW 3 (Continued)

#3	Cherries, 8 piece set on rack	$ 15.00-	18.00

ROW 4:

#1	Herbs, 8 piece set (3 missing here), complete	15.00-	18.00
#2	Scottie dogs, 3 piece range set	18.00-	20.00
#3	Daisy, 4 piece set on rack	8.00-	10.00

ROW 5:

#1	Dutch set, 6 piece, not Tipp City	15.00-	20.00
#2	Basket, 4 piece set on rack	10.00-	12.00
#3	Dutch, 3 piece set in box	8.00-	10.00

Page 181

ROW 1:

#1,2	Lady salt or pepper	$ 10.00-	12.50
#3,4	Same, flour or sugar	15.00-	17.50
#5,6	Jadite, ea.	10.00-	12.50
#7,8	"Art Deco", pr.	20.00-	24.00
#9,10	Blue, pr.	18.00-	22.00
#11,12	Fired-on blue, pr.	10.00-	12.00

ROW 2:

#1	Fired-on Dutch set	25.00-	30.00
#2	Dutch white set	12.00-	15.00
#3	Lady watering set (goes with Row 2 on previous page)	25.00-	30.00

ROW 3:

#1	Singing birds set	$ 20.00-	25.00
#2,3	Scotty dogs, ea.	6.00-	7.50
#4	Rooster set	10.00-	12.50
#5,6	"Sombrero Sam" set	22.00-	25.00
#7,8	White set w/salt dehumidifier	10.00-	12.50

ROW 4:

#1,2	Black set (w/good lettering)	18.00-	20.00
#3,4	Uncle Sam's hat set	8.00-	10.00
#5,6	Kitchen cabinet shakers (maybe powdered sugar?), ea.	12.00-	15.00
#6-9	Floral or cherry, pr.	8.00-	10.00

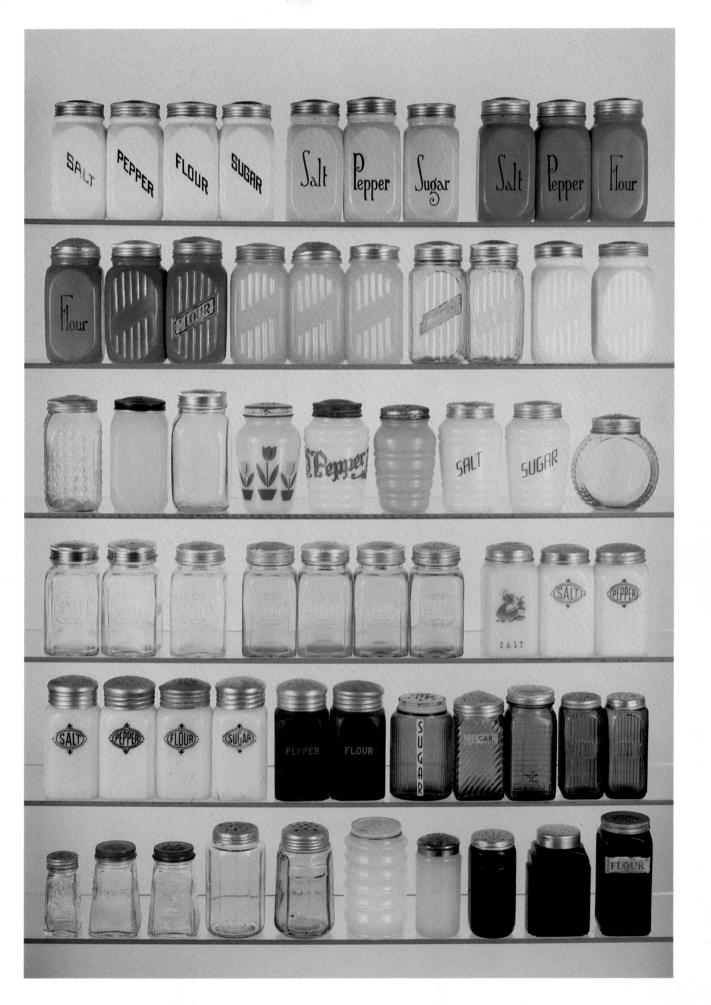

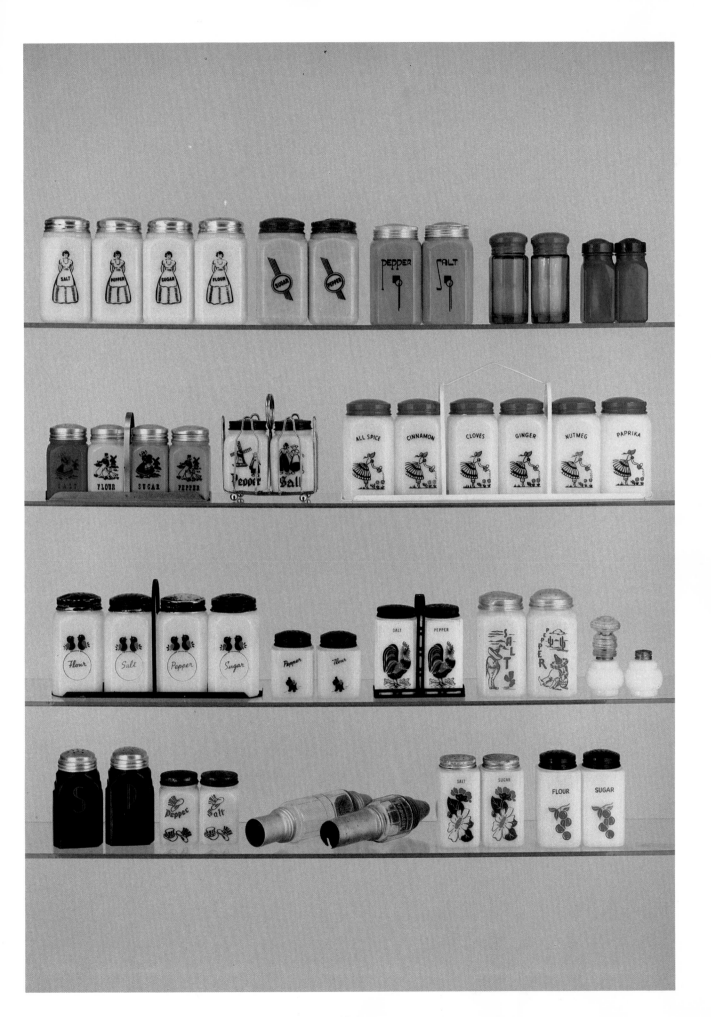

SHAKERS JEANNETTE, McKEE ETC.

JEANNETTE GLASS COMPANY (first 4½ rows)
Page 183
ROW 1:

#1,2 Delphite blue, 8 oz., salt or pepper, ea.	$10.00-	12.50
#3,4 Same, sugar or paprika	18.00-	20.00
#5,6 Jadite, decorated salt or pepper	10.00-	12.50
#7,8 Same, mouth wash or bicarbonate soda	25.00-	30.00
#9,10 Jadite, 6 oz. w/o label, ea.	4.00-	5.00

ROW 2:

#1-4 Jadite light, 8 oz., shaker	8.00-	10.00
#5 Jadite dark, pepper	9.00-	11.00
#6 Same, flour	11.00-	13.00
#7,8 Delphite blue, square, salt or pepper	12.00-	15.00
#9 Same, flour or sugar (p.23)	20.00-	25.00

ROW 3:

#1,2 Jadite dark, square, salt or pepper	11.00-	13.00
#3,4 Same, flour or sugar	13.00-	16.00
#5,6 Jadite light, square, salt or pepper	8.00-	10.00

ROW 3 (Continued)

#7,8 Same, flour or sugar	$ 10.00-	12.00
#9 "Jennyware" pink	18.00-	20.00

ROW 4:

#1-4 "Jennyware" ultra-marine (subtract $1.00 missing label), ea.	20.00-	22.00
#5-8 Same, crystal	6.00-	8.00

ROW 5:

#1-4 "Jennyware" flat shaker, ea.	25.00-	28.00
#5 Same, crystal	18.00-	20.00
#6 Green, sold as sugar shaker	30.00-	40.00
#7 Unknown manufacturer, green "Zipper"	25.00-	30.00
#8 Green, plain	30.00-	35.00

ROW 6:

#1 Green, embossed flour	35.00-	40.00
#2 Crystal, embossed salt	15.00-	18.00
#3 Crystal, embossed all spice	15.00-	18.00
#4 Crystal, embossed cinnamon	15.00-	18.00
#5 Crystal, ribbed	8.00-	10.00
#6-11 Sneath green, ea.	22.00-	25.00

McKEE "Roman Arch" Shakers
Page 184
ROW 1:

#1 Skokie Green, salt	$ 18.00-	20.00
#2-4 Same, pepper, flour or sugar	12.00-	15.00
#5 Same, cinnamon	22.00-	25.00
#6,7 Delphite blue, salt or pepper	25.00-	30.00
#8-10 Fired-on colors, ea.	7.00-	9.00

ROW 2:

#1-4 & 7-9 "Dots" green or red, ea.	11.00-	14.00
#5,6 Same, blue	15.00-	17.00
#10 Custard w/green flour	8.00-	10.00

ROW 3:

#1-4 Custard w/black lettering	8.00-	10.00
#5,6 "Diamond Check", pr. on white	25.00-	30.00

ROW 3 (Continued)

#7,8 "Dots" on white, pr.	$ 18.00-	20.00
#9,10 Fired-on red, pr.	15.00-	18.00

ROW 4:

#1-4 White w/black, ea.	6.00-	8.00
#5-7 White w/red, ea.	9.00-	11.00
#8,9 Crystal, frosted, ea.	6.00-	7.00

ROW 5:

#1-11 Black, salt ($10.00-12.00) all others w/good lettering	8.00-	10.00
Black w/o lettering	5.00-	6.00

ROW 6:

#1-4 Fired-on colored set	15.00-	18.00
#5 "Bow", red on white	10.00-	12.00
#6-9 "Ships", ea.	6.00-	8.00

McKEE "Square" Shakers
Page 185
ROW 1:

#1-3 Large, 16 oz., ea.	$ 25.00-	30.00
#4-7 Small, 8 oz., ea.	4.00-	5.00
#8,9 Skokie Green, pr.	20.00-	25.00

ROW 2:

#1,2 Embossed dark jade salt or pepper	28.00-	30.00
#3,4 Same, flour or sugar	30.00-	35.00
#5 Embossed Chalaine blue, flour $40.00-45.00; others	55.00-	60.00
#6-9 Chalaine blue, ea.	22.50-	25.00

ROW 3:

#1-4 White, ea.	7.00-	9.00
#5-8 "HOTPOINT" or "ELECTROCHEF" embossed white, ea.	6.00-	8.00
#9,10 White, ea.	5.00-	7.00

ROW 4:

#1-7 Skokie Green light or dark, ea.	$ 8.00-	10.00
#8 Same, "Cinnamon"	22.00-	25.00
#9,10 Black w/o good lettering ($8.00-10.00 ea.) w/lettering, ea.	10.00-	12.50

ROW 5:

#1-4 Custard, ea.	8.00-	10.00
#5-6 Same, ginger, cinnamon, nutmeg w/good lettering, ea.	18.00-	20.00
#8-10 Seville yellow, ea.	8.00-	10.00

ROW 6:

#1-4 Seville yellow, ea.	10.00-	12.50
#5-8 Skokie Green, dark, ea.	8.00-	10.00

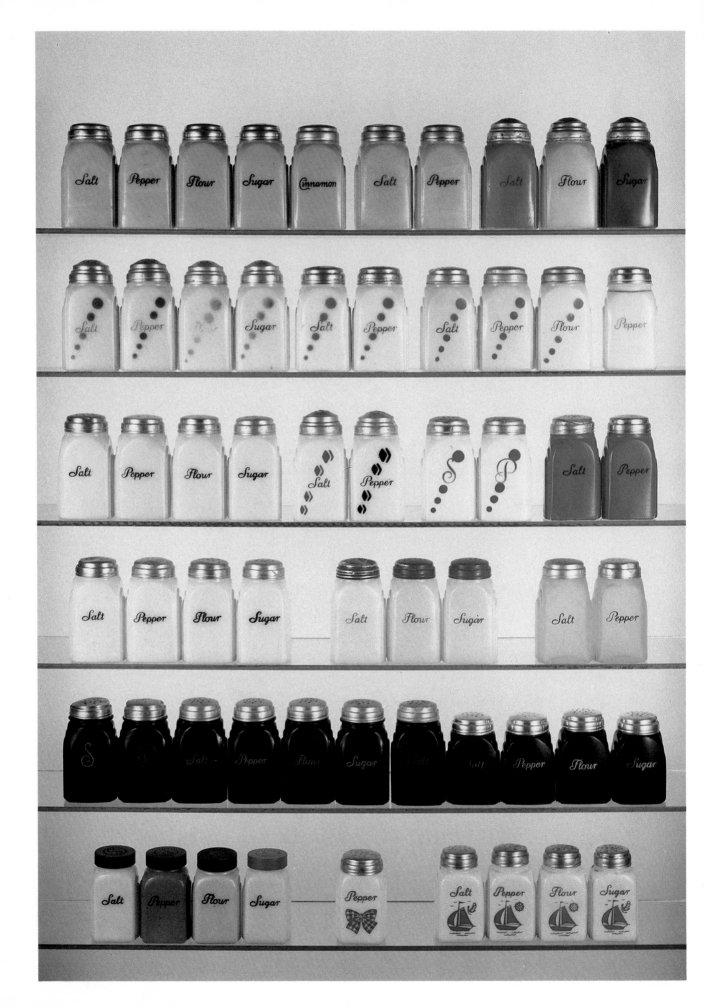

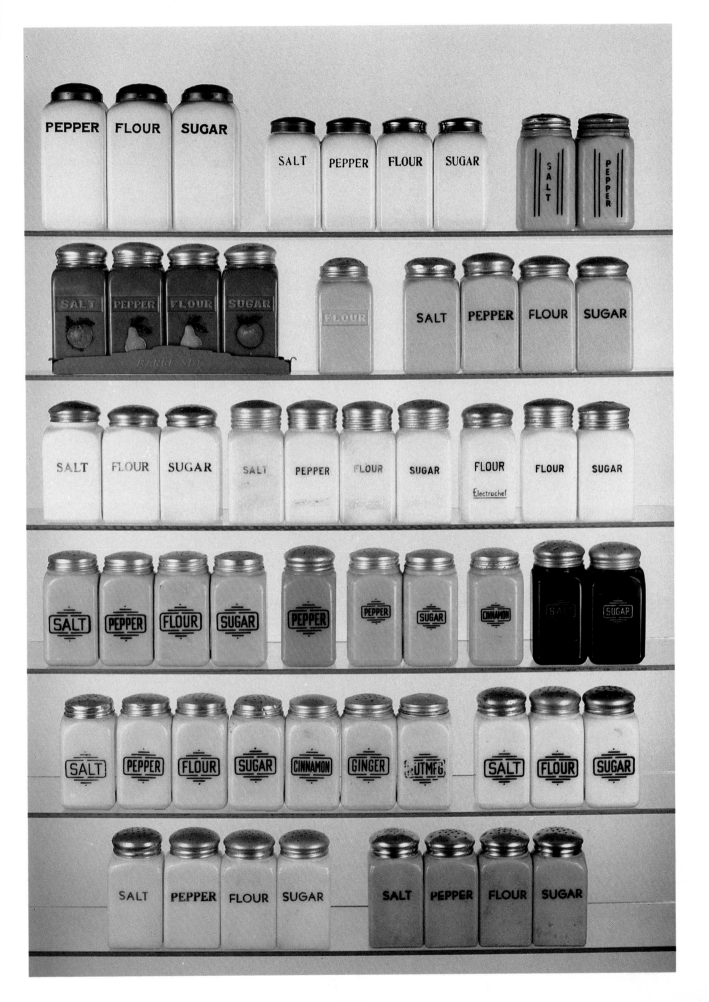

STRAW HOLDERS

These are memory-laden items from the past. (Remember the ice cream chairs and tables at the drug store and reaching for a straw for the cherry coke or milk shake from the straw holder in the center of the table?) However, whether you do or not, today's collectors, with their 2.5 children, are finding these items remarkably adaptable to everyday life because said children LOVE to drink from straws--- milk particularly goes down better with one. So, the ice cream parlor straw holder from bygone days is finding new life at the kitchen table or counter and is being snapped from the market.

Colored straw holders or ones with a particular pattern are premier finds; however, some people are very satisfied to just find the clear glass one of their memory.

ROW 1:	#1	Crystal w/o top, Heisey	$ 85.00-100.00
		Same, w/glass top	150.00-175.00
	#2	Green w/top	300.00-325.00
	#3	Crystal w/top	60.00- 65.00
	#4	Crystal "Pattern" glass/glass top	175.00-200.00
	#5	Crystal w/top	55.00- 65.00
	#6	Green w/etching w/top	300.00-350.00
ROW 2:	#1	Green w/top	250.00-275.00
	#2	Crystal w/o top, Heisey "Greek Key"	125.00-150.00
		Same, w/glass top	250.00-275.00
	#3	Green, English Hobnail, vase or straw holder	85.00- 95.00
	#4	Crystal, blown, w/top	55.00- 65.00
	#5	Pink, Imperial or Cambridge vase, used as straw holder	65.00- 75.00
	#6	Crystal, blown, w/top	60.00- 70.00
ROW 3:	#1	Crystal, marked FLORENCE, w/top	60.00- 70.00
	#2	Crystal, w/top	55.00- 65.00
	#3	Crystal, Fostoria "American," vase or straw holder, w/o lid	80.00- 95.00
	#4	Green w/top	250.00-275.00
	#5	Crystal, still made as Barber shop equipment	25.00- 35.00
	#6	Crystal, w/top (sm. straws/Dr.'s tongue depressor)	25.00- 30.00
BELOW	#1	Cobalt blue, 12″ high w/top (used as straw holder but has been questioned as to validity by several collectors)	150.00-200.00
	#2,3	Red or peacock blue, 9¼″ (late 1950's or early 1960's)	150.00-200.00
	#4	Blue or amber (not shown), (older than Depression era)	175.00-225.00
	#5	Crystal, w/painted flowers (older than Depression era)	75.00- 85.00
	#6	Fostoria "American" w/lid	210.00-235.00

SUGAR SHAKERS

How about those new discoveries of cobalt blue, black, yellow and ultra-marine sugar shakers!

Page 189
ROW 1:
#1,2 Cambridge #732, pink (ewer cream $30.00-35.00)	$100.00- 115.00
#3,4 Cambridge #732, green (tall ewer cream $30.00-35.00)	105.00- 120.00
#5 Cambridge, blue	115.00- 135.00
#6,7 Cambridge, amber (syrup w/cover $40.00-45.00)	65.00- 85.00

ROW 2:
#1,2 Cambridge, pink (ewer cream $20.00-25.00)	65.00- 85.00
#3 Cambridge, amber, crystal foot and glass top	75.00- 90.00
#4,5 Same, pink (ewer cream $22.00-25.00)	85.00- 100.00
#6,7 Heisey "Yeoman", pink (cream $20.00-25.00); (add $10.00-15.00 w/glass top)	65.00- 75.00
#8 Cobalt blue	125.00- 150.00
#9 Green, w/green screw-in top	125.00- 145.00

ROW 3:
#1,2 Green or pink, footed ("Tilt-a-spoon")	150.00- 175.00
#3,4 Green, 2 shades, possibly Paden City	110.00- 115.00
#5 Same, cobalt blue	200.00- 250.00

ROW 3 (Continued)
#6 Same, amber	$100.00- 125.00
#7 Paden City, pinched in, amber	95.00- 115.00
#8 Same, green	85.00- 100.00

ROW 4:
#1 Green, Hocking	50.00- 65.00
#2 Green, Hocking	45.00- 55.00
#3 Unknown	40.00- 45.00
#4 Green, "Hex Optic"	85.00- 100.00
#5 Amber	45.00- 55.00
#6 Unknown, pink	55.00- 65.00
#7 Pink, w/red top	85.00- 100.00
#8 Paden City "Party Line", pink	65.00- 75.00

ROW 5:
#1 Crystal, Paden City, 2 part dispenser	15.00- 18.00
#2 Crystal, L.E. Smith	30.00- 35.00
#3 Crystal, "West Sanitary Automatic Sugar"	20.00- 25.00
#4,5 Crystal, Hazel Atlas and unknown, ea.	10.00- 12.50
#6 Crystal, faintly marked "Czechoslovakia"	20.00- 25.00

Page 190
ROW 1:
#1 Lancaster Glass Co. "Beehive", green	$125.00- 150.00
#2-7 "Bullet" shape made by both Jeannette and Paden City	
#2,3 Green	85.00- 100.00
#4 Yellow	150.00- 175.00
#5 Pink	85.00- 100.00
#6 Crystal	18.00- 25.00
#7 Pink	100.00- 115.00

ROW 2:
#1,2 Blue, pink "Monroe Mfg. Co., Elgin Ill., Pat Pend."	150.00- 200.00
#3,4 Green or pink, footed	85.00- 100.00
#5 Green	100.00- 125.00

ROW 3:
#1 Jeannette, light jade	45.00- 55.00
#2-4 Same, pink decorated, green or yellowish jade, ea.	$40.00- 50.00
#5-7 Jeannette, pink or green	30.00- 40.00
#6 Same, frosted pink	35.00- 40.00
#8 Green, cone top	55.00- 65.00

ROW 4:
#1 White Clambroth	35.00- 37.50
#2,3 Green or pink	18.00- 20.00
#4-6 Orange, forest green or red (late 50's or 60's), ea.	45.00- 60.00
#7 Amber, horseshoe pattern	35.00- 40.00
#8 Green, older style	20.00- 25.00
#9 Crystal, marked sugar and cinnamon	12.00- 15.00

Page 191
ROW 1:
#1 "Bullet", ultra-marine	$175.00- 200.00
#2 Same, crystal	15.00- 18.00
#3 Same, emerald green	100.00- 125.00
#4 Green	85.00- 100.00
#5,6 Crystal, "Beehive" or cone	20.00- 25.00

ROW 2:
#1 Pink, footed	75.00- 85.00
#2 Same, green	80.00- 90.00
#3 Same, crystal	14.00- 16.00
#4 Same, black	175.00- 200.00
#5 Same, SCA	50.00- 65.00
#6 Same, amber	85.00- 110.00

ROW 3:
#1 Jeannette, dark jade	50.00- 60.00
#2 Same, pink	35.00- 40.00
#3,4 Jeannette "Hex Optic", green or pink	85.00- 100.00
#5 Paden City "Rena", Line 154, green or pink	85.00- 100.00

ROW 4:
#1,2 Heisey, pink or green	$85.00- 100.00
#3 Same, crystal	45.00- 50.00
#4 Pink measured teaspoon	85.00- 95.00
#5 Crystal	14.00- 18.00
#6 Red fired-on	12.50- 15.00
#7 Blue	50.00- 65.00

ROW 5:
#1 Paden City "Rena", Line 154, individual sugar, crystal	12.00- 15.00
#2 Amber, individual sugar	40.00- 50.00
#3 Owens-Illinois, forest green	8.00- 10.00
#4 Green	50.00- 65.00
#5 Green, handled (possibly Pattern Glass syrup)	60.00- 75.00
#6 Crystal, decorated w/flowers	12.00- 15.00
#7 Blue, marked "Made in Japan" (New!)	5.00- 10.00

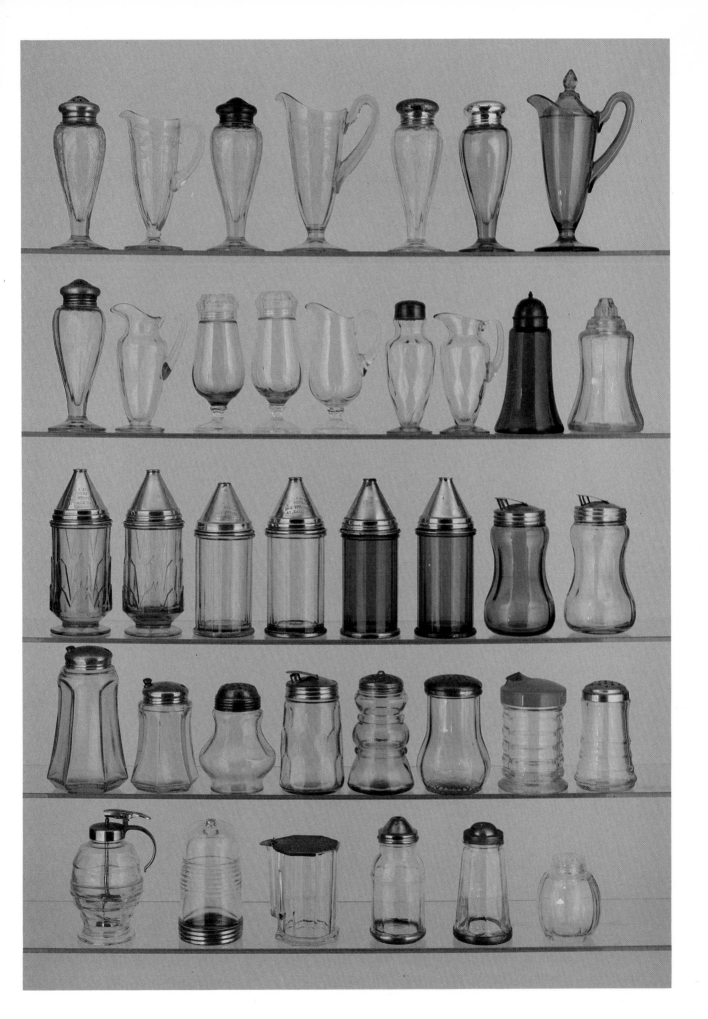

SYRUP PITCHERS

I've often remarked on the fact that many Depression Glass collectors are "item" collectors; however, the number of people I'm encountering in my travels who collect only syrup pitchers is amazing even to me. Somewhere in the course of their conversation, they generally speak of what attractive displays the pieces make in their homes and how fascinating they find the various shapes. I particularly remember one man, a farmer, who seemed rather shy and hesitant until he began speaking of his interest in syrup pitchers. His weathered face, eyes and voice suddenly were transformed into the soft, glowing enthusiasm of a connoisseur. Depression glass. . . the stuff dreams are made of?

ROW 1:	#1	Cambridge, w/cover, amber	$40.00- 45.00
	#2	Same, green	50.00- 55.00
	#3	Paden City, green	25.00- 30.00
	#4	Imperial, w/slotted lid, pink	55.00- 65.00
	#5	Same, amber	50.00- 65.00
ROW 2:	#1	Hazel Atlas, pink	40.00- 45.00
	#2	Same, green	15.00- 17.50
	#3	Same, pink	40.00- 45.00
	#4	Hazel Atlas, pink	37.50- 42.50
	#5	Hazel Atlas green	35.00- 40.00
	#6	Same, pink	37.50- 42.50
ROW 3:	#1,2	Fostoria "Mayfair", green or pink w/underliner	55.00- 65.00
	#3	Fostoria "Chintz"	50.00- 60.00
	#4	Fostoria "Mayfair", yellow w/underliner	55.00- 65.00
	#5	Same, amber	50.00- 60.00
ROW 4:	#1	Pink	40.00- 45.00
	#2	Green w/liner	40.00- 50.00
	#3	Imperial, pink	45.00- 50.00
	#4	Imperial, pink w/floral cutting	40.00- 45.00
	#5	Same, green, plain	40.00- 45.00
ROW 5:	#1	Paden City #198, 8 oz., amber	40.00- 50.00
	#2	Same, green	30.00- 35.00
	#3	Same, pink	30.00- 35.00
	#4	Paden City "Party Line", green	32.50- 37.50
	#5	Same, pink	32.50- 35.00
	#6	Paden City #198, 12 oz., green w/liner	40.00- 45.00

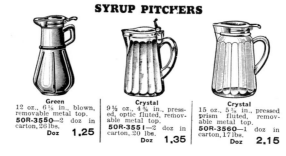

SYRUP PITCHERS

Green
12 oz., 6⅛ in., blown, removable metal top.
50R-3550—2 doz in carton, 26 lbs.
Doz 1.25

Crystal
9½ oz., 4¾ in., pressed, optic fluted, removable metal top.
50R-3551—2 doz in carton, 20 lbs.
Doz 1.35

Crystal
15 oz., 5⅜ in., pressed prism fluted, removable metal top.
50R-3560—1 doz in carton, 17 lbs.
Doz 2.15

SYRUP PITCHERS Continued

ROW 1: #1   Crystal $10.00- 12.50
    #2   Green (possibly U.S. Glass)   30.00- 35.00
    #3   Standard Glass, pink   30.00- 35.00
    #4   Hocking, green swirl   35.00- 38.00
    #5,6   Crystal, ea.   8.00- 10.00

ROW 2: #1   Amber/yellow combination w/glass lid   40.00- 45.00
    #2   Pink w/green knob, handle and pink underliner   40.00- 50.00
    #3   Duncan & Miller "Caribbean", blue   75.00- 85.00
    #4   Same, crystal   35.00- 45.00
    #5   Cambridge, amber   30.00- 35.00

ROW 3: #1   Paden City, green floral cutting w/underliner   30.00- 35.00
    #2   Same, pink   32.50- 37.50
    #3   Same, pink w/painted flowers   35.00- 40.00
    #4   Cambridge, pink   30.00- 35.00
    #5   McKee, forest green   25.00- 30.00

ROW 4: #1,3   Cambridge etched design w/underliner, pink   50.00- 60.00
    #2   Same, green   45.00- 55.00
    #4   Same, amber   45.00- 50.00
    #5   Cambridge, etched "Cleo"   75.00- 85.00

ROW 5: #1   Cambridge, "Tally Ho" amber   50.00- 60.00
    #2   Cambridge, pink   45.00- 55.00
    #3   Same, amber   40.00- 50.00
    #4   Cambridge, amber   45.00- 50.00
    #5   Crystal, with crystal top   15.00- 18.00
    #6   Black   40.00- 50.00

ROW 6: #1   Heisey, "Moongleam" green   50.00- 65.00
    #2   Heisey, "Sahara" yellow   60.00- 75.00
    #3   Same, crystal   35.00- 40.00
    #4   Heisey, "Flamingo" pink   40.00- 45.00
    #5   Same, "Moongleam" green   45.00- 50.00
    #6   U.S. Glass miniature syrup, crystal   50.00- 60.00

TOILETRIES

The sets on the top row with the hand painted, enameled flowers are very desirable. However, these same black topped pieces can be found without any decoration and bring about one fifth the price of the decorated sets.

Soap dishes, porcelain hooks and other accoutrements of the bathroom per se are just beginning to interest collectors. Finding things in like colors is some problem.

ROW 1:	#1-4,6,7	Bathroom items, ea.	$25.00- 30.00
	#5	Tumbler, 10 oz.	12.00- 15.00
	#8,9	Jars, ea.	5.00- 6.00
ROW 2:	#1	2 bottles on black amethyst tray	12.00- 15.00
	#2	3 green bottles on green tray	70.00- 85.00
	#3	Green apothecary jar (ALCOHOL)	30.00- 35.00
	#4	Pink (HAND LOTION)	30.00- 35.00
	#5,6	White Fenton bottles, ea.	15.00- 17.00
	#7	Soap dish, embossed "Holton Soap saver"	15.00- 17.00
ROW 3:	#1,2	Jeannette bottles (bath powder?), ea.	25.00- 30.00
	#3	Pink bottle	20.00- 22.00
	#4	English Hobnail "MOUTHWASH" bottle	25.00- 30.00
	#5	Frosted pink soap dish	18.00- 20.00
	#6	White soap dish	10.00- 12.00
	#7	Amber soap dish	15.00- 18.00
ROW 4:	#1	Bath set on black tray	45.00- 50.00
	#2-4	White bottles, hand painted blue Hollyhocks, ea.	8.00- 10.00
	#5	Frosted pink toothbrush holder	18.00- 20.00
	#6,7	Blue or jadite wall cup holders	15.00- 17.00
ROW 5:	#1,2	Coaster, ea.	6.00- 8.00
	#3	Combination tumbler and toothbrush holder, white	12.00- 15.00
	#4-6	Toothbrush holders, blue	22.50- 25.00
		White	15.00- 18.00
		Jadite	20.00- 22.50
ROW 6:	#1-3	Soap dish, blue	18.00- 20.00
		White	8.00- 10.00
		Jadite	15.00- 18.00
	#4-7	Towel hooks, large, white or Jadite	10.00- 12.00
		Same, small	8.00- 10.00

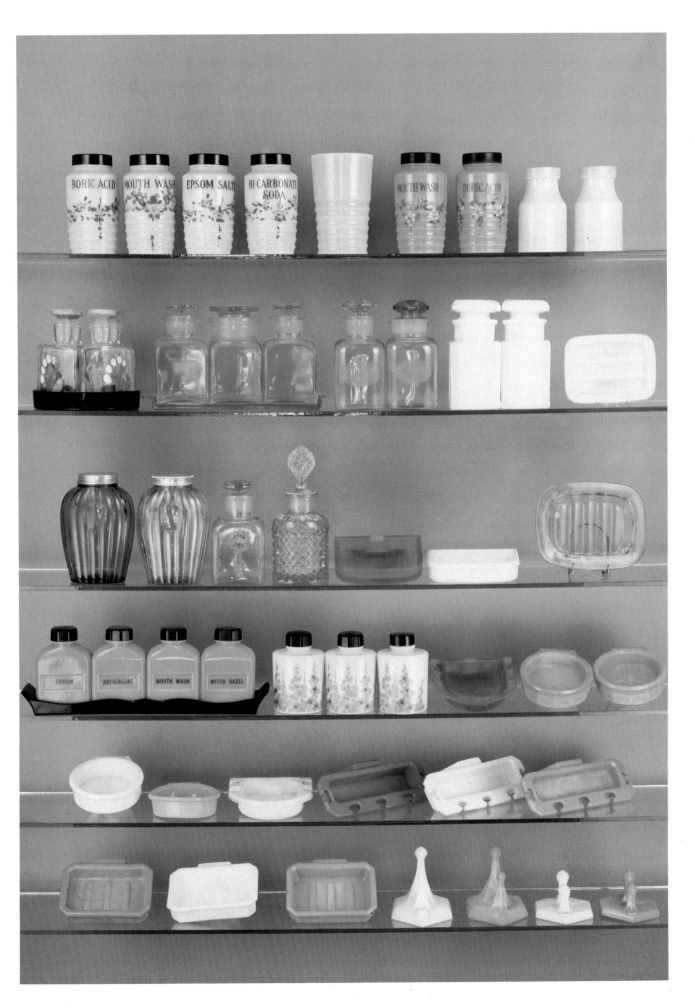

WATER BOTTLES

The use of water bottles has gone the way of ice boxes. Today, you stick your glass in the door of the refrigerator to get ice or water instead of opening it. There are numerous other bottles throughout the book so I have only included some common ones that you can find without too much difficulty. The only ones that are a problem to find are the oddly colored ones such as amber, red, or cobalt blue.

The McKee beverage dispenser below sells at $50.00-60.00.

ROW 1:	#1	"Water Falls"	$ 12.00- 15.00
	#2	"Water"	8.00- 10.00
	#3	"G.E." shows old refrigerator	12.00- 15.00
	#4	"Well", amber	30.00- 40.00
	#5	"Ships"	12.00- 15.00
ROW 2:	#1	Owens-Illinois "Juice" on one side and "Water" on other	3.00- 5.00
	#2	Forest green "Penguin"	12.00- 15.00
	#3	Lattice design w/lid	35.00- 45.00
	#4	Hocking "Royal Ruby"	40.00- 50.00
	#5	"G.E. round	6.00- 8.00
ROW 3:	#1	"Crisscross", crystal	4.00- 5.00
	#2	"The Well Informed Choose Ice Refrigeration"	8.00- 10.00
	#3	"Beveragette", Pat. 1919	10.00- 12.00
	#4	Cobalt blue, 64 oz., 10″ tall	50.00- 55.00
	#5	Same, 32 oz.	30.00- 35.00

PART 3 PATTERNS & COMPANIES

"CRISSCROSS," HAZEL ATLAS GLASS COMPANY, 1936-1938

Collectors have been collecting kitchenware by colors more than they have been collecting by patterns since publication of the last book. This has meant that there have not been as dramatic a price change in "Crisscross" in the last few years as there had been previously. The exceptions to that rule are the green water bottles and newly discovered pieces. A few pink tumblers have surfaced with one collector in Texas having accumulated eleven in his set. No tumblers in blue have been reported to go with the pitcher and no pitcher in pink has been found to go with the tumblers. Collectors of Depression Glass have been familiar with problems such as these for years.

The creamers and sugars with lids remain elusive, but they are available with persistent searching. Note that I have removed the cobalt blue lemon reamer from the listing as no one has been able to prove its existence so far. The 5½" round refrigerator bowl with cover in green and pink are probably the next most difficult pieces to find in those colors except for the lemon reamer in pink. One of these days we will find out why some items were produced in limited quantites, but for now we can only wonder.

The cobalt color still attracts many admirers, but the demand in recent months has been for the other colors. This creates a steady market for dealers except for the extremely common green and crystal reamers. Some one did a fantastic marketing promotion years ago on those reamers. I doubt if they will ever be hard to find in our lifetime!

	BLUE	CRYSTAL	GREEN	PINK
Bottle, water, 32 oz.	$ ----	$ 3.00- 14.00	$75.00- 80.00	$ ----
Bottle, water, 64 oz.	----	4.00- 5.00	85.00- 95.00	----
Bowl, mixing set (5)	105.00- 125.00	30.00- 40.00	62.00- 75.00	62.00- 75.00
Bow, mixing, 6⅝"	12.00- 14.00	3.00- 4.00	8.00- 10.00	8.00- 10.00
Bowl, mixing, 7⅝ "	14.00- 16.00	4.00- 5.00	10.00- 12.00	10.00- 12.00
Bowl, mixing, 8¾"	18.00- 20.00	6.00- 7.00	14.00- 16.00	14.00- 16.00
Bowl, mixing, 9⅝"	14.00- 16.00	6.00- 7.00	10.00- 12.00	10.00- 12.00
Bowl, mixing, 10⅝"	50.00- 60.00	12.00- 15.00	20.00- 25.00	20.00- 25.00
Butter, ¼ lb.	40.00- 45.00	6.00- 8.00	30.00- 35.00	30.00- 35.00
Butter, 1 lb	55.00- 65.00	8.00- 9.00	20.00- 25.00	20.00- 25.00
Creamer	----	4.00- 5.00	20.00- 25.00	12.00- 15.00
Food mixer (baby face)	----	20.00- 25.00	----	----
Pitcher, 54 oz.	500.00- 600.00	50.00- 60.00	----	----
Reamer, lemon	----	3.00- 5.00	8.00- 10.00	225.00- 275.00
Reamer, orange	150.00- 165.00	3.00- 5.00	8.00- 10.00	150.00- 200.00
Refrigerator bowl, round				
5½" w/cover	----	3.00- 4.00	40.00- 50.00	40.00- 50.00
Refrigerator bowl, w/cover				
4" x 4"	18.00- 20.00	2.00- 3.00	12.00- 15.00	8.00- 10.00
4" x 8"	50.00- 55.00	3.00- 4.00	20.00- 22.00	15.00- 18.00
8" x 8"	60.00- 70.00	4.00- 5.00	30.00- 35.00	40.00- 45.00
Refrigerator dish, (like butter)				
3½" x 5¾"	60.00- 70.00	10.00- 12.00	30.00- 35.00	----
Sugar	----	10.00- 12.00	18.00- 20.00	20.00- 25.00
Sugar lid	----	10.00- 12.00	25.00- 30.00	25.00- 30.00
Tumbler, 9 oz.	----	12.00- 15.00	----	40.00- 50.00

"DOTS," McKEE GLASS COMPANY, 1930's THROUGH EARLY '40's

McKee issued this as a "Deluxe" line of kitchenware and sold items to merchants for the princely sums of four to twelve dollars per dozen! Collectors are searching high, low, long and hard to find some of these dotted goodies for their kitchens. The dots, red being most popular, appear also in blue, green, black and yellow according to data and are to be found on "white opal" or "French ivory" backgrounds. As you can tell from the picture, very little "Dots" is found in colors other than red; and the black, though attractive, is the least popular color with collectors at the moment. Perhaps black and white kitchen decor was a '30's exclusive?

Some collectors are buying blue dot pieces and incorporating them with their delphite blue collections.

	RED/GREEN DOTS on CUSTARD	BLUE DOTS on CUSTARD	DOTS on WHITE
Bowl, 9", scalloped edge	$22.00- 25.00	$25.00- 27.00	$15.00- 18.00
Bowl, 9" w/spout	20.00- 22.00	22.00- 25.00	12.00- 15.00
Bowl, drippings	22.00- 25.00	25.00- 27.00	15.00- 18.00
Bowl, egg beater w/lip	15.00- 18.00	18.00- 20.00	10.00- 12.00
Butter dish	75.00- 85.00	75.00- 85.00	30.00- 35.00
Canister, 48 oz., screw-on lid	30.00- 35.00	35.00- 40.00	25.00- 30.00
Canister, 28 oz., screw-on lid	27.00- 30.00	30.00- 35.00	20.00- 25.00
Canister & lid, round, 48 oz.	18.00- 20.00	20.00- 22.00	15.00- 18.00
Canister & lid, round, 40 oz.	16.00- 18.00	18.00- 20.00	12.00- 15.00
Canister & lid, round, 24 oz.	14.00- 16.00	16.00- 18.00	10.00- 12.00
Canister & lid, round, 10 oz.	14.00- 15.00	16.00- 18.00	10.00- 12.00
Mixing bowl, 9"	12.00- 14.00	15.00- 18.00	8.00- 10.00
Mixing bowl, 8"	10.00- 12.00	12.00- 15.00	7.00- 8.00
Mixing bowl, 7"	8.00- 10.00	10.00- 12.00	6.00- 7.00
Mixing bowl, 6"	7.00- 8.00	8.00- 10.00	5.00- 6.00
Pitcher, 2 cup	22.50- 25.00	25.00- 30.00	20.00- 22.50
Refrigerator dish, 4" x 5"	10.00- 12.00	8.00- 10.00	6.00- 8.00
Refrigerator dish, 5" x 8"	12.00- 14.00	18.00- 20.00	10.00- 12.00
Shaker, ea.	11.00- 14.00	14.00- 17.00	8.00- 10.00

"DOTS," McKEE, HAZEL ATLAS, HOCKING GLASS COMPANIES, '30's, '40's, '50's

As you may gather, dotted kitchenware was popular enough to have several companies plying their designs in the market place. The tumblers on the second row, though inexpensive, aren't that easily found; and in Row 3, the cover to the drippings jar has been elevated to show its "drippings" label. The Hocking pieces on the bottom row are more easily found today at markets and shows due to their having been marketed as late as the 1950's. The demand for these 50's pieces has risen dramatically.

Page 206, ROW 1:

#1-3 McKee round canisters, 40 oz.	$16.00- 18.00	
Same, 24 oz.	14.00- 16.00	
Same, 10 oz.	14.00- 15.00	
#4 McKee, bowl, 10"	12.00- 14.00	
#5 McKee, 2 cup pitcher	18.00- 20.00	

ROWS 2-4 ALL HAZEL ATLAS
ROW 2:

#1 Covered round refrigerator bowl	15.00- 18.00	
#2 Stack set	15.00- 17.50	
#3 Pitcher, 2 cup	18.00- 20.00	
#4-6 Tumblers, 10 oz., ea.	3.00- 4.00	

ROW 3:

#1,2 Mixing bowl set (5)	25.00- 30.00	
9" (shown in Row 4)	8.00- 9.00	
8"	6.00- 7.00	
7" (not shown)	5.00- 6.00	

ROW 3 (Continued)

	6"	$ 4.00-	5.00
	5" (shown in Row 4)	3.00-	4.00

ROW 4:

#1-3	Mixing bowls (priced in Row 3)		
#4	Butter dish	40.00-	45.00

ROW 5:

#1,6	Hocking mixing bowl set (4)"Polka Dots"	16.00-	22.00
	9½"	5.00-	6.50
	8½"	4.00-	5.50
	7½" (not shown)	4.00-	5.50
	6½" (not shown)	3.00-	4.50
#2,4,5,7	Shakers, ea.	3.00-	4.00
#3	Grease jar	6.00-	8.00

FIRE-KING (LATE), HOCKING GLASS COMPANY, LATE 40's, EARLY 1950's

Hocking issued these mixing bowl/range sets in sundry designs; but the tulip designs were then, and are now, the most popular. The Jad-ite and ivorine refrigerator and stove items are presently less desirable. Actually, they're in lesser supply than are the earlier "Sapphire" blue Fire-King pieces which collectors are fast removing from the market place! The company originally guaranteed this ovenware from breakage for two years from purchase. Many collectors find it still very serviceable.

Page 207, ROW 1:

#1-3 Mixing bowl set (4)-"Kitchen Aids"	$24.00- 28.00	
9½"	8.00- 9.00	
8½"	6.00- 7.00	
7½"	5.00- 6.00	
6½" (not shown)	4.00- 5.00	

ROW 2:

#1-3 Range set (3) Same as above	20.00- 25.00	
Grease jar	12.00- 15.00	
Shakers, ea.	4.00- 5.00	
#4-6 Range set (3)-"Tulips"	16.00- 20.00	
Grease jar	8.00- 10.00	
Shakers, ea.	4.00- 5.00	

ROW 3:

#1-3 Mixing bowl set "Tulips"	16.00- 22.00	

ROW 3 (Continued)

	9½"	$ 5.00-	6.50
	8½"	4.00-	5.50
	7½" (not shown)	4.00-	5.50
	6½"	3.00-	4.50

ROW 4:

#1	Skillet, jad-ite	15.00-	20.00
	Same, blue	100.00-	120.00
#2	Refrigerator dish, 4" x 8"	4.50-	5.00
#3	Butter dish, ¼ lb.	8.00-	10.00

ROW 5:

#1	Ivory pie plate, 8⅜"	3.00-	3.50
#2	Ivory cereal bowl	.75-	1.00
#3	Ivory custard	.50-	.75
#4	Federal ovenware stack set	12.00-	15.00

FIRE-KING

Page 209

ROW 1: #1 "Swedish Modern", "Turquoise Blue" 11″ mixing bowl, 3 qt. $ 6.00- 7.50
       #2 Same, 9½″, 2 qt. 5.00- 6.50
       #3 Same, 8″, 1 qt. 4.00- 5.50
       #4 Same, 6½″, 1 pt. 3.00- 4.50

ROW 2: #1 "Splash Proof", "Turquoise Blue", 9½″ mixing bowl, 4 qt. 6.00- 7.50
       #2 Same, 8½″, 3 qt. 5.00- 6.50
       #3 Same, 7½″, 2 qt. 5.00- 6.50
       #4 Same, 6½″, 1 qt. 3.00- 4.50

ROW 3: #1 "Splash Proof", "Fruit", 9½″ mixing bowl, 4 qt. 5.00- 6.50
       #2 Same, 8½″, 3 qt. 4.00- 5.50
       #3 Same, 7½″, 2 qt. 4.00- 5.50
       #4 Same, 6½″, 1 qt. 3.00- 4.50

ROW 4: #1 "Ivory" 9⅛″ deep loaf pan 5.00- 7.50
       #2 Same, 6 oz. individual baker 1.00- 1.50
       #3 Same, 9″ cake pan 8.00- 10.00
       #4 Same, 10½″ baking pan 7.00- 9.00

ROW 5: #1 Jad-ite juice saver pie plate, 10⅜″ 25.00- 30.00
       #2 Mug w/design on outside (no design $2.00-3.00) 12.00- 15.00
       #3 Jade-ite mixing bowl, 8″ or 9″ (not shown) 3.00- 5.00
       #4 Same, 7″ or 6″ (not shown) 2.00- 3.00

FIRE-KING SAPPHIRE BLUE

Page 210,211

Baker, 1 pt., round or square	$ 3.50- 4.00	Custard cup, 5 oz.	$ 2.00- 3.00
Baker, 1 qt.	4.50- 5.00	Custard cup, 6 oz., 2 styles	2.50- 3.50
Baker, 1½ qt.	8.50- 9.00	Loaf pan, 9⅛″, deep	15.00- 18.00
Baker, 2 qt.	9.00- 10.00	Nurser, 4 oz.	10.00- 12.00
Bowl, 5⅜ ″, cereal, or deep dish pie plate	7.00- 9.00	Nurser, 8 oz.	10.00- 12.00
Bowl, 4⅜ ″, individual pie plate	7.00- 9.00	Pie plate, 8⅜″	6.00- 7.00
Bowl, 16 oz. measuring, 2 spout	12.00- 15.00	Pie plate, 9″	7.00- 8.00
Cake pan (deep), 8¾″	10.00- 12.00	Pie plate, 9⅝″	8.00- 9.00
Casserole, 1 pt., knob handle cover	8.00- 10.00	Pie plate, 10⅜,″ w/juice saver rim	45.00- 50.00
Same, 1½ qt.	9.00- 10.00	Perculator top, 2⅛″	3.00- 3.50
Same, 1½ qt.	10.00- 12.00	Refrigerator jar & cover, 4½″x5″	7.00- 9.00
Same, 2 qt.	12.00- 15.00	Same, 5⅛″ x 9⅛″	12.00- 15.00
Casserole, individual, 10 oz.	10.00- 12.00	Roaster, 8¾″	25.00- 30.00
Casserole, 1 qt., pie plate cover	10.00- 12.50	Roaster, 10⅜″	40.00- 50.00
Same, 1½ qt.	12.00- 15.00	Table server, tab handles (hot plate)	10.00- 12.00
Same, 2 qt.	15.00- 18.00	Utility bowl, 6⅞″	6.00- 7.50
Coffee mug, 7 oz., 2 styles	16.00- 18.00	Utility bowl, 8⅜″	7.00- 8.50
Cup, 8 oz., dry measure, no spout	40.00- 50.00	Utility bowl, 10⅛″	10.00- 12.00
Cup, 8 oz. measuring, 1 spout	10.00- 12.00	Utility pan, 8⅛″ x 12½″	12.00- 15.00
Cup, 8 oz. measuring, 3 spout	12.00- 15.00		

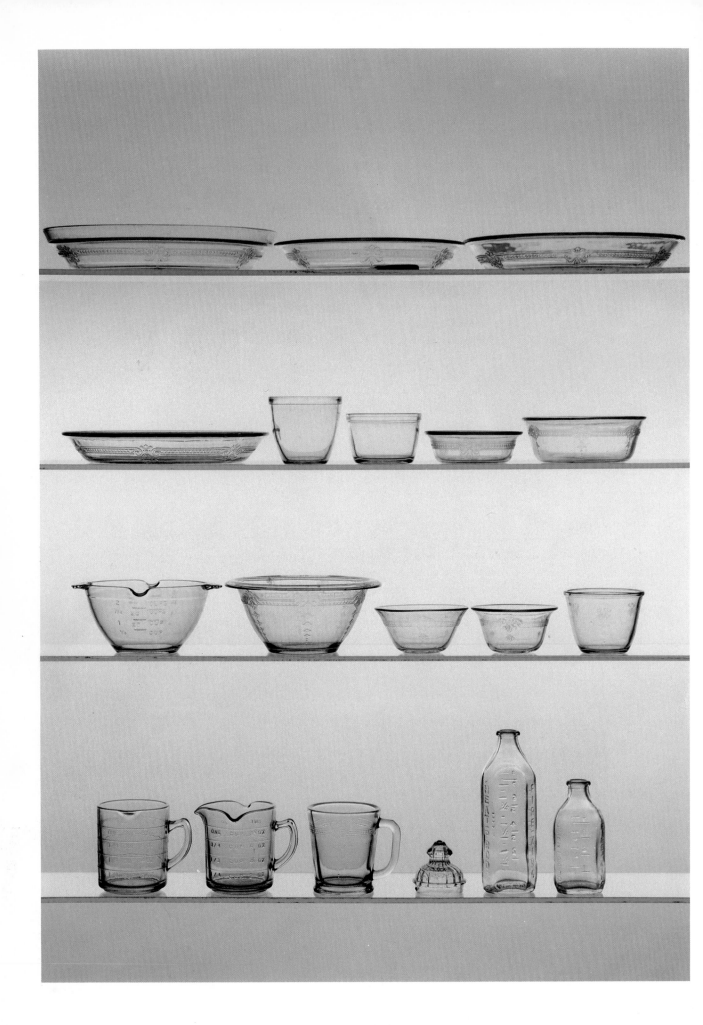

FRY GLASSWARE, FRY GLASS COMPANY, 1920's

You'll never encounter any more avid collectors than those who collect "Fry" glassware! It's distinguished mostly by its translucent, opaline, almost luminescent color; and more often than not, the sixty-year-old pieces you do find will have some damage.

Page 213

ROW 1:	#1	Utility pitcher	$ 75.00-	85.00
	#2	Foval teapot w/cobalt handle and knob	125.00-	150.00
	#3	Stacking refrigerator set (6 pieces)(as shown $25.00)	55.00-	65.00
ROW 2:	#1,2	Utility jar, ea. w/lid	25.00-	30.00
	#3	Measure cup	30.00-	35.00
	#4	Reamer	30.00-	35.00
ROW 3:	#1	Divided 3 part relish	22.00-	25.00
	#2	Green covered casserole	75.00-	85.00
	#3	Covered casserole in metal holder	28.00-	30.00
ROW 4:	#1	Rectangular casserole, 9½"x 5¼"	25.00-	28.00
	#2	Refrigerator dish, 8"x 8"	30.00-	32.00
	#3	Grill plate	10.00-	12.00
ROW 5:	#1	Meat platter	30.00-	35.00
	#2	Refrigerator dish w/floral design, 7¾" sq.	25.00-	28.00.

FRY GLASSWARE and "S and R" GLASS, 1920; SEARS & ROEBUCK ADVERTISED GLASSWARE, 1940's

Collectors are calling the flower and leaf designed ovenware sold by Sears and Roebuck in the 1940's "S and R" glass. Sears advertised this line in their 1946 catalogue under the name "Maid of Honor."

Page 214

ROW 1	#1	Reamer, pink	125.00-	175.00
	#2	Popcorn popper	35.00-	45.00
	#3	Reamer, vaseline	35.00-	45.00
		Same, embossed w/ad ("BAKE-RITE...Cinn. Ohio")	150.00-	200.00
ROW 2:	#1	Drawer tray, 6 part	12.00-	14.00
	#2	Refrigerator dish, 9½" x 5½"	12.00-	15.00
	#3	Refrigerator dish, deep, 4" x 4"	10.00-	12.00
ROW 3:	#1	Stack set, w/lids	22.00-	25.00
	#2	Pie plate	10.00-	12.00
	#3	Cup	18.00-	20.00
		Saucer (not shown)	4.00-	5.00
	#4	Custard cup	3.00-	4.00
ROW 4	#1,2	"S & R" roaster, lid on right (14" x 8½" x 6½")	35.00-	45.00
ROW 5:	#1	"S & R" bean pot w/lid, 2½ pt.	10.00-	12.00
	#2	"S & R" baker, open	4.00-	5.00
		Same, w/lid	7.00-	8.00
	#3	"S & R" loaf pan	12.00-	15.00
	#4	"S & R" custard cup, 4 oz.	1.00-	1.50

FRY GLASSWARE, FRY GLASS COMPANY; GLASBAKE, RANGE-TEK, ETC., McKEE GLASS CO.

Page 215

ROW 1:	#1	Glasbake, tea kettle, white	40.00-	45.00
	#2	Same, coffee pot	30.00-	35.00
	#3	Same, unusual style	40.00-	45.00
	#4	Rectangular casserole, probably made for Westinghouse	7.00-	10.00
ROW 2:	#1	Glasbake, jello mold	5.00-	7.50
	#2	Same, rectangular casserole	6.00-	8.00
	#3	Same, tube cake pan	10.00-	12.50
ROW 3:	#1	"Safe Bake", Saben Glass Co., heart shape 9½" or 10½"	6.00-	8.00
	#2	"Flamex" teapot	8.00-	10.00
	#3	Same, double boiler	15.00-	20.00
ROW 4:	#1	Same as #1 in Row 3, 8½" casserole	12.00-	15.00
	#2	Same, 6½"	3.50-	4.50
	#3	Glasbake, 4¼" square	3.00-	4.00
	#4	Same, 4¼" x 8"	6.00-	8.00

"JENNYWARE," JEANNETTE GLASS COMPANY, 1936-1938

"Jennyware" is quite popular with collectors, due, in part, to the many different items that can be acquired. Collectors of the ultra-marine color should be aware of color variations due to various batches of glass or to color "burnout" as result of imprecise temperature controls.

The decanter shown in the top row was made by Imperial Glass Company but is being collected with "Jennyware". It sells for $40.00-45.00 in ultra-marine but only $15.00-20.00 in green.

	CRYSTAL	PINK	ULTRA-MARINE
Page 217,218			
Bowl, mixing set (3)	$18.00-25.00	$65.00-70.00	$70.00- 90.00
Bowl, 10½"	7.00-10.00	30.00-32.00	30.00- 40.00
Bowl, 8¼"	6.00- 8.00	18.00-20.00	25.00- 30.00
Bowl, 6"	4.00- 6.00	18.00-20.00	16.00- 20.00
Butter dish, deep bottom	20.00-25.00	60.00-65.00	75.00- 85.00
Butter dish, flat bottom	----	----	150.00-175.00
Coaster	----	5.00- 6.00	5.00- 6.00
Measuring cup set (4)	50.00-65.00	75.00-90.00	90.00-105.00
1 cup	15.00-20.00	25.00-30.00	32.00- 35.00
½ cup	15.00-20.00	25.00-30.00	32.00- 35.00
⅓ cup	10.00-12.50	12.50-15.00	15.00- 20.00
¼ cup	10.00-12.50	12.50-15.00	11.00- 15.00
Pitcher, 36 oz.	20.00-25.00	50.00-65.00	70.00- 75.00
Reamer	60.00-75.00	50.00-65.00	60.00- 75.00
Refrigerator dish, 70 oz., round	8.00-10.00	30.00-35.00	30.00- 35.00
Refrigerator dish, 32 oz., round	6.00- 8.00	15.00-18.00	16.00- 18.00
Refrigerator dish, 16 oz., round	4.00- 6.00	18.00-20.00	18.00- 20.00
Refrigerator dish, 4½" x 4½"	4.00- 6.00	12.00-14.00	14.00- 16.00
Refrigerator dish, 4½" x 9"	6.00- 8.00	20.00-22.00	22.00- 24.00
Shaker, footed, ea.	6.00- 8.00	18.00-20.00	20.00- 22.00
Shaker, flat, ea.	18.00-20.00	25.00-28.00	----
Tumbler, 8 oz.	18.00-20.00	25.00-30.00	30.00- 35.00

PYREX CORNING GLASS WORKS

The boxed glassware shown here was discovered in early 1986 near Chicago. It is great to find new information; so keep looking and you might make a "find" too.

Page 219

ROW 1:	#1	Pyrex 8 piece "Matched Set" #145 consisting of six 5 oz. custard cups, one 1½ qt. casserole w/pie plate cover in box	$18.00- 22.00
	#2	Pyrex 9 piece "Economy Set" #179 consisting of 8 oz. measuring cup, 9½" pie plate, six 4 oz. custards and handy cup rack	20.00- 25.00
ROW 2 and items 1 & 2 in Row 3:		Pyrex "Gift Set" #245 consisting of 8½" pie plate, 9⅛" loaf pan, 8⅝" cake dish, 10½" utility dish, six 4 oz. custards, and 1½ qt. casserole in box	30.00- 35.00
ROW 3:	#3	Blue, 4¼" x 6¾" w/lid	25.00- 30.00
	#4	Blue, milk pitcher	25.00- 30.00
ROW 4:	#1	Mixing bowl set, 6½", 7½", 8½"	12.00- 15.00
	#2	Divided relish	10.00- 12.50
	#3	Teapot, with floral cutting (marked "Corning Pyrex") in lid	35.00- 50.00

"SHIPS," McKEE GLASS COMPANY, 1930's

I might point out that the pitcher shown in the top row is not a part of the set, but it is a great "go-with" accessory. It sells for $20.00-25.00. Collectors still prefer the white lids for their canisters; but if you use these, the clear tops are much more convenient for viewing the contents of the dish!

Page 221

Bowl, drippings, 8 oz.	$22.00- 25.00		Mixing bowl, 9″	$ 10.00- 12.00
Bowl, drippings, 16 oz.	22.00- 25.00		Mixing bowl, 8″	8.00- 10.00
Bowl, drippings, rectangular (4″ x 5″)	22.00- 25.00		Mixing bowl, 7″	7.00- 8.00
Bowl, egg beater, 4½″	18.00- 20.00		Mixing bowl, 6″	5.00- 6.00
Butter dish	18.00- 20.00		Pitcher, 2 cup	12.00- 15.00
Canister & lid, round, 48 oz., 5″h.	16.00- 18.00		Refrigerator dish, 4″ x 5″	9.00- 10 00
Canister & lid, round, 46 oz., 4½″h	14.00- 16.00		Refrigerator dish, 5″ x 8″	12.00- 15.00
Canister & lid, round, 24 oz., 3½″h	12.00- 14.00		Shaker, ea.	6.00- 8.00
Canister & lid, round, 10 oz., 2½″h	10.00- 12.00		Tumbler (or Egg Cup)	10.00- 12.00
Mixing bowl set (4)	30.00- 36.00			

VITROCK, HOCKING GLASS COMPANY, LATE 1930's

Page 222

ROW 1:

#1,2 Oval refrigerator set (3)*	$45.00- 50.00	
Same, 8″	15.00- 20.00	
Same, 7″	12.50- 15.00	
Same, 6″ (not shown)	12.50- 15.00	
#3 Cannister, 20 oz. screw lid		
w/label	12.00- 15.00	
w/o label	10.00- 11.00	
#4-6 Shakers w/label	5.00- 7.00	
#7 Reamer embossed Vitrock	15.00- 18.00	
Same, not embossed	8.00- 12.00	

ROW 2:

#1,2 Decorated bowl	8.00- 10.00	
Same, 5¼″	4.00- 5.00	
#3 Refrigerator dish, 4″ x 4″	8.00- 10.00	
Same, 4″ x 8″ (not shown)	15.00- 20.00	
Same, 8″ x 8″	22.00- 25.00	
#4 Reamer, 2 piece	22.00- 25.00	

ROW 3:

#1,2 Mixing bowls, 7½″	$ 3.00- 4.00	
6¾″	4.00- 5.00	
#3,5 Shakers (priced in Row 1)		
#4 Grease jar	12.00- 15.00	
#6 Ash tray w/o ad	5.00- 6.00	
w/ad (Lancaster Eagle-Gazette 1809-1937)	10.00- 12.00	

ROW 4:

#1-3 Mixing bowls as in Row 3, 11½″	12.00- 14.00	
Same w/ad (Bertman Pickle Co.)	22.00- 25.00	
10¼″	12.00- 15.00	
9½″	8.00- 10.00	
8½″ (not shown)	6.00- 7.00	

*Add $2.00 for fired-on colors of blue or red

LATE ARRIVALS

As always happens, when you think you have covered everything and shown all you can, another piece or two is discovered. In any case there is a mixture of everything here including some previously omitted toiletries.

In closing this book, I wish you luck in finding your GLASSWARE!

Page 223

ROW 1:	#1	Fostoria, white syrup	$ 15.00- 18.00
	#2	1 cup dry measure w/reamer top, crystal	25.00- 28.00
	#3,4	"Narc_____Bath Salt made by Richard Hudnut, N.Y., Paris"	25.00- 30.00
	#4,5	Hazel Atlas cobalt blue shakers	25.00- 30.00
	#6	Blue shaker, Pat. Applied Apr. 3, 88	20.00- 25.00
ROW 2:	#1	Doorknobs, chalaine blue	50.00- 60.00
	#2	Bulldog cotton ball dispenser	25.00- 30.00
	#3	Shaving mug	40.00- 50.00
	#4	Shaving mug, "Matthews" MFGWU, Pat. Oct. 3, 22	60.00- 75.00
	#5	Red "Ten To One" razor hone, Made in USA, Pat Pend	20.00- 25.00
	#6	Green, "Lillicrap's Hone, Made in England"	15.00- 20.00
ROW 3:	#1	White, "McKee Glass Safety Razor Hone" Pat Applied For	12.00- 15.00
	#2	Same, custard	18.00- 20.00
	#3	Black, "All-Blade Safety Razor Sharpener" Pat. Pending	18.00- 22.00
	#4	Same, cobalt blue	25.00- 30.00
	#5	Same, ultra-marine	22.00- 25.00
	#6	Same, light green	18.00- 22.00
	#7	Crystal, "Clix Blades, Clix Always Clicks"	18.00- 20.00
	#8	Same, pink	22.00- 25.00
ROW 4:	#1	Ice cream set, cobalt blue	50.00- 65.00
	#2,3	Cobalt bath bottle, "Des Pat 'M' in circle R.D. No. 82″, ea.	20.00- 25.00
	#4	Apothecary jar, cobalt blue	35.00- 45.00
	#5	Fry casserole (Dutch shoe emblem on base)	22.00- 25.00
ROW 5:	#1	Vitrock canister, 47 oz. w/lid	25.00- 30.00
	#2	Fenton pitcher, jade (tray $30.00-35.00; tumbler $10.00-12.00)	100.00- 125.00
	#3	Same, lilac w/tray (tumbler $12.00-15.00)	150.00- 200.00

Publications I recommend:

Books by Gene Florence

Collectors Encyclopedia of Depression Glass	$19.95
Pocket Guide to Depression Glass	$9.95
Collectors Encyclopedia of Occupied Japan I	$12.95
Collectors Encyclopedia of Occupied Japan II	$14.95
Collectors Encyclopedia of Occupied Japan III	$19.95
Elegant Glassware of the Depression Era	$19.95

Add $1.00 postage for the first book, $.35 for each additional book.

Copies of these books may be ordered from:

Gene Florence
P.O. Box 22186
Lexington, KY 40522

or

COLLECTOR BOOKS
P.O. Box 3009
Paducah, KY 42001